Living S

Living Skillfully

Buddhist Philosophy of Life from the Vimalakīrti Sūtra

DALE S. WRIGHT

OXFORD
UNIVERSITY PRESS

Oxford University Press is a department of the University of Oxford. It furthers the University's objective of excellence in research, scholarship, and education by publishing worldwide. Oxford is a registered trade mark of Oxford University Press in the UK and certain other countries.

Published in the United States of America by Oxford University Press
198 Madison Avenue, New York, NY 10016, United States of America.

© Oxford University Press 2021

Library of Congress Cataloging-in-Publication Data
Names: Wright, Dale Stuart, author.
Title: Living skillfully : Buddhist philosophy of life from the
Vimalakīrti Sūtra / Dale S. Wright.
Description: New York : Oxford University Press, 2021. |
Includes bibliographical references and index.
Identifiers: LCCN 2021034553 (print) | LCCN 2021034554 (ebook) |
ISBN 9780197587355 (hardback) | ISBN 9780197587379 (epub)
Subjects: LCSH: Tripiṭaka. Sūtrapiṭaka.
Vimalakīrtinirdeśa—Commentaries. | Religious life—Buddhism. |
Buddhists—Conduct of life. | Spiritual life—Buddhism.
Classification: LCC BQ2217 .W75 2021 (print) |
LCC BQ2217 (ebook) | DDC 294.3/85—dc23
LC record available at https://lccn.loc.gov/2021034553
LC ebook record available at https://lccn.loc.gov/2021034554

DOI: 10.1093/oso/9780197587355.001.0001

1 3 5 7 9 8 6 4 2

Printed by Sheridan Books, Inc., United States of America

Contents

Acknowledgments

I owe the motivation for this book to my former students at Occidental College. As soon as they sensed that I might be willing to teach it, they made clear to me that what they wanted most from my instruction on Buddhism was something practical, something worthwhile that could be applied in their lives. Standing at the threshold of adult life, they were able to see the startling difference between lives that appeared to be well lived and those that just weren't. They wanted me to teach them what Buddhism had to say about lives skillfully lived—theirs, not just someone else's. They wanted a Buddhist philosophy of life that could be tested in their own lives here and now.

While I did my best to honor that request for something useful, I knew that I could only provide that through the traditions of Buddhism as we have inherited them from numerous Asian cultures. To get what they wanted, my students would have to bite the bullet of reading strange and difficult texts and of considering ways of thinking and living that at face value would inevitably seem foreign and inapplicable.

As it turned out, the most difficult and most lucrative "bullet" that they would be challenged to bite was the *Vimalakīrti Sūtra*. On first reading they found it incomprehensible and therefore uninspiring. What they needed from me was some way to get it into existential view, some way to understand it in relation to the lives they were living. This book is the outcome of my decades-long effort to meet those needs, and I can't begin to tell all of you how grateful I am for having been forced to do that. If any clarity or inspiration made its way through that process and into this book, I owe it to the demands my students put on me. In appreciation, I dedicate this book to all of them.

But, of course, my debts extend far beyond that. I have thanked supportive family and friends in earlier writing, but I still want to repeat here that none of this would have been possible without them.

Thanking is insufficient. As Vimalakirti would have said, we are inextricably linked, we are "non-dual."

I am grateful for thoughtful editorial and publishing assistance from colleagues at Oxford University Press, to Cynthia Read and others with whom I have enjoyed a long-standing productive relationship. Their expertise and professional demeanor make the task of writing all that much easier.

Finally, allow me to thank in person a number of friends whose friendship on this occasion took the form of reading and commenting on this manuscript prior to publication: William Edelglass, Steven Heine, David James, John Kelly, Karen King, David Klemm, Malek Moazzam-Doulat, Sam Mowe, D. Keith Naylor, Martha Ronk, and Furyu Nancy Schroeder. Their insights and comments helped shake out my dogmatism and get this book down to the business at hand. In profound appreciation!

Introduction

Skillful Living

Buddhist writings invariably emphasize one crucial point: that living a good life, a healthy, undeluded life that is wide awake to the realities it faces, depends on the development of certain skills. And so it seems. The people we tend to admire are skillful in the ways they go about living their lives—in the way they confront problems that arise, in the effective choices they often make, and in their openness to new ideas and people. They are skillful in their capacity to speak and act constructively in their communities, in their lack of resentment and self-absorption, in the ways they encourage and support others, and in their disciplined ability to work hard toward worthwhile goals. These skills and many others are vital, the keys that make it possible to flourish in life. Buddhist texts often emphasize how being intelligent and knowing a lot, while certainly helpful, are not the same as being skillful in life—nor are they as effective in awakening us from unhealthy, self-destructive ways of living.

Calling certain ways of living "skillful" and others "unskillful" implies that these are capacities that can be cultivated, skills that can be acquired through practice. Although some people might seem to have more or less innate talent for a particular skill, or were raised in a way that emphasized and reinforced that skill, the development of skill is a possibility open to anyone and everyone. And they are always matters of degree. Just as you can be more or less skillful as a cook, a musician, or a rock climber, your capacity to avoid self-destructive choices or to effectively calm and transform the fires of your own internal anger will be more or less developed. The distinction between skills that are weak, adequate, or excellent can be substantial, and this can make all the difference in real-life situations. Fortunately, these capacities can

Living Skillfully. Dale S. Wright, Oxford University Press. © Oxford University Press 2021.
DOI: 10.1093/oso/9780197587355.003.0001

be cultivated through practice. Although practice doesn't ever make "perfect," it almost always makes "better."

There are serious obstacles to the acquisition of these crucial life skills, however. From a Buddhist point of view, the deadliest of these obstacles are called the "three poisons," three internal threats that stand in the way of our leading good lives. We consume these "poisons" whenever we succumb to (1) greed or insatiable, self-obsessed craving, not just for things but for security, praise, love—anything; (2) aversions like hatred, rejection, or closure toward whatever seems unpleasant, threatening, or out of the ordinary; and (3) delusions that tragically lead us to misunderstand both the situations we face in life and who we really are. Greed, hatred, and delusion poison our efforts to face up to the challenges of life and lure us into adopting ineffective life strategies that are doomed to exacerbate the suffering that gave rise to these poisonous tendencies in the first place.

These obstacles to skillful, effective living aren't just troublesome for some of us. We all share them—every one of us—to various degrees and in our own specific ways. For some they manifest as fear and retreat in life, for others as arrogant, unregulated self-assertion, for others as self-doubt, habitual withdrawal into daydreams, steady undercurrents of brooding anxiety, boredom and restlessness, childish bragging, deep levels of discontent, addictions to eating or drinking, insatiable thirst for sexual fulfillment—we could keep this list of our common weaknesses going for pages.

The metaphor of "poison" is perfectly apt because from the very beginning Buddhists had conceived of life not as a battle between good and evil or between sin and obedience but rather in terms of healthy and unhealthy ways of living. Framing the central issues in life in these terms reorients our approach. The Buddha imagined his role not predominantly as a philosopher, mystic, prophet, or warrior against evil but instead as a physician, a healer. He believed that through his own inner explorations practical remedies for the fundamental maladies of human existence had come to light and that these healing prescriptions were now openly available to anyone interested in pursuing them. The Buddhist teachings are therefore framed as a set of therapeutic practices strategically designed to initiate this process of healing. They begin in meditative self-observation to diagnose obstructive patterns that prevent flourishing in life, and they come to fruition in practices designed to replace destructive habits with skillful patterns of living conducive to a healthy life of open awareness, wisdom, and compassion. The basic Buddhist insight is that if much suffering is self-caused through habitual maladaptive behavior, then much suffering can also be alleviated through the intentional development of a skillful life of health and awareness.

Buddhist Philosophy of Life

Socrates said that philosophy—literally, the "love of wisdom"—gets started in the first place by the human experiences of awe and wonder. In awesome moments of life and in pensive acts of wondering, we sometimes find ourselves face-to-face with big questions. Why are things the way they are? How in fact are they really, once we place our ordinary assumptions in question? And how should we live our lives in view of this reality? Although Western philosophies evolved over the centuries away from these initiating experiences of awe and wonder toward subdisciplines of inquiry like logic and theories of knowledge, the underlying pursuit of wisdom in life continued to rise to the surface, on occasion evoking awe and wonder.

Although Buddhist philosophy includes reflection in each of those areas of thought, its primary motivating issue is what Zen Buddhists call "the great matter of life and death." What is it to live as a human being, and what kinds of lives are possible for us? And to some extent it must also be true in Buddhism that this inquiry gets motivated or at least pushed along by experiences of awe and wonder. Descriptions of awesome and pensive experiences can be found throughout Buddhist writings. Overwhelmingly, though, what initiates Buddhist reflection and its paths of practice are the underlying experiences of human suffering in correlation with prescriptive questions about healthy life practices that mitigate destructive tendencies.

Dukkha is the Buddhist word that we translate as "suffering." But this word is much broader and more encompassing than our word "suffering." Beyond the pain of sickness, injury, and misfortune, *dukkha* encompasses the dull anxiety of everyday life as well as the despair that surfaces in self-doubt or lack of motivation. It includes a full range of human dissatisfactions—boredom, listlessness, feelings of fear, ignorance, inadequacy, isolation, and loneliness—from the trivial to the most devastating.

Dukkha is what eats away at our inner constitution, tempting us to indulge in desperate, shortsighted remedies that turn out to have poisonous effects. Even pulling back cautiously from the front edge of life for fear of suffering is just more *dukkha*. Questions about the significance of human suffering and how best to face this pervasive experience without turning away from it in denial and delusion—these are what motivate not just Buddhist philosophy but every aspect of the Buddhist dharma, its teachings and practices. That is what Buddhism purports to be about and that is why in this book I opt to call it "philosophy of life." It is a pursuit of wisdom correlated directly to the lives we live.

Early Buddhists recognized that there are two distinct sources of suffering in life. One of these is that the world out there just keeps hammering away at us: injuries, losses, and illnesses caused by unexpected changes, slippery surfaces, thieves, viruses, insults, and humiliations. Human beings are limited in physical and cognitive capacity, and the world is an enormous, complex rush of change and contingency. Although we certainly try, we can't ever control it. We are overwhelmed in the turbulence and pace of reality, and the result is that our troubles never entirely go away. The second source of suffering resides in our patterns of reaction to this overwhelming reality, the ways we respond to an uncontrollable world. There are unhealthy, ineffective responses and healthy, skillful ones.

An early Buddhist scripture has the Buddha teach a parable about the sources of suffering. He says that if we are hit by an arrow, that would be painful. But if we then respond to that pain inappropriately— by exaggerating its harm, by wallowing in self-pity, by obsessively recounting the incident in a way that builds mental anguish to higher and higher levels—those additional wounds would be self-inflicted. This suffering is caused not by the world being the way it is but by our being the way we are. As the Buddha puts it, it is as though we continue to shoot the arrows of suffering at ourselves long after the first one coming from the world brought us some level of pain.

The first of these arrows is the unavoidable effect of life itself. Even those who are very good at avoiding mistakes and dodging injuries will not escape unharmed. There will be blood. We will all make mistakes, we will all get sick, we will all be diminished by aging, and, against every fragment of our willpower, we will all be ruthlessly eliminated by the powers of death. What Buddhist philosophy of life asks is, given that the world just is this way, and given that both joy and pain are inevitable parts of life, what would a healthy, insightful response to the sheer fact of this reality be? What skills would help us respond to the "first arrows" in life without adding suffering to that pain through misguided, maladaptive reactions? How are we to live skillfully in a world of inevitable pain and joy, in a world that is always—if our eyes are open at all—awesome and overwhelming?

Buddhist responses to this fundamental question begin in a refusal to promise a heavenly afterlife in another world. Instead they call upon us to face the realities before us with honesty, understanding, and conviction, to acknowledge the human situation, and to resist tendencies to soothe ourselves with self-centered illusions. Rather than promising imaginary consolations for the difficulties of life, envisioning heavenly realms after death where life would not be like this, Buddhist approaches attempt to face up to the life we have as it is and to develop the skills to live successfully right where we are. The desire to become invulnerable and immortal in heaven reveals an underlying desire to get out of life, a death wish condemning the very life we are already living. It encourages us to imagine living another kind of life in some other world rather than focusing on being who we actually are in the world that is right before our eyes. For Buddhists, this imaginary escape is delusion, the third and most serious of the "poisons" that seriously undermine the quality of our lives.

In view of these realities, the primary Buddhist recommendation is the cultivation of skills for living that are based on clarity of vision and steadfast mental training and that help us avoid ingesting the poisons of greed, hatred, and delusion. The metaphor Buddhists employ for this way of living is that of a "path"—or, more accurately, a set of paths pioneered by others—that can be explored by anyone hoping to respond to life's challenges with greater wisdom and skill in living. The central image of a path began with the Buddha's "middle path," a way forward that avoids extremes that can do severe damage to our prospects of living skillfully. It received further clarity through the Buddhist "eightfold path," which names particular areas of life that are amenable to development through life-changing practices. There have been many versions and reformulations of paths that provide guidance and direction for Buddhists. One sacred text for Buddhists, the *Vimalakīrti Sūtra*, offers several images of worthwhile paths and in so doing shows how different kinds of people in different circumstances and settings can benefit from wiser, more skillful ways to address the facts of life.

The *Vimalakīrti Sūtra*

The Buddhist philosophy of life that we develop in this book draws inspiration from the *Vimalakīrti Sūtra*, a Buddhist text that dwells at great length and in unique ways on the theme of skillful living. Sutras are sacred writings that intend to communicate the teachings of the Buddha—the dharma. The earliest Buddhist sutras were memorized accounts of what the Buddha taught on some particular occasion, or an amalgamation of teachings from a talk that he had repeated on numerous occasions. These early sutras are quite brief and relatively simple in form and content, often including numbered lists of important ideas or practices, and thus not overly difficult to memorize. Their point was to articulate the most important elements of a philosophy of life that could be put into practice and embodied in real-life situations.

As India transitioned from an oral culture to a literary one through the first five centuries of Buddhist history, the sutras were gradually committed to writing. Although centuries had passed since the life of the Buddha himself, sutras articulating these teachings continued to be composed. The later a sutra's composition date, the more likely that it would be longer and more sophisticated in literary form, more elaborate in imagery and teaching, and less confined to the earliest format of the dharma. All things change and evolve, as the Buddha's teachings explain to us, and that is certainly true of Buddhist writings.

The *Vimalakīrti Sūtra*, which will guide our reflections on skillful living, is an early Mahayana Buddhist text written in Sanskrit probably just after the beginning of the Common Era and is closely linked by the similarity of its teachings to the foundational Perfection of Wisdom sutras being composed at roughly that same time. The sutra circulated throughout northern Buddhist cultures for many centuries primarily in several early Chinese and Tibetan translations. When Buddhism disappeared from India after thriving there for many centuries, all Sanskrit copies of the sutra appeared to have been lost. Miraculously, however, a recent discovery in the deepest chambers of the Potala Palace in Tibet now gives us a Sanskrit version of the sutra to contemplate.

Of the hundreds of Buddhist texts I've read throughout my life, this one is my favorite. Here's why. First, although the *Vimalakīrti Sūtra* begins, like all others, as an account of what the Buddha taught on some occasion, it quickly transitions in an altogether different direction by telling the story of another Buddhist, a layperson named Vimalakirti. Vimalakirti isn't just described; he is praised and valorized as the most "enlightened" of all Buddhists, second only to the Buddha himself. This was an outrageous assertion in India at that time. Although people who were not monks or nuns could be Buddhists in some derivative sense, the serious quest for Buddhist enlightenment was thought to require a lifelong monastic commitment. Monks and occasionally nuns were thought to experience "awakening," but not ordinary householders, not the laity. The image of Vimalakirti as a profoundly awakened layperson was therefore a very important turning point in the history of Buddhism. It opened Buddhism in ways that are still coming to light.

Moreover, Vimalakirti is imagined in the sutra not as a reclusive householder, frequently isolated in meditation and protected from the chaos of society. He is a husband, a father, a homeowner, a businessperson, a landlord, a political activist, a fully engaged reformer, and someone who truly enjoys his life. Vimalakirti is as worldly as you can get. Developing this image of Vimalakirti as a revolutionary break with the monastic monopoly on Buddhist achievement, the author of the sutra has two of the most prominent monks in the narrative exclaim to the Buddha in astonishment: If Vimalakirti can be this wise and exalted, they ask, "who is there who would not conceive the spirit of unexcelled, perfect enlightenment?" (27). In that sentence the sutra asserts in no uncertain terms that the ultimate goal of Buddhism is an open possibility for any human being, as perhaps it had been in the mind of the Buddha himself.

Our second reason for featuring this Buddhist text, related to its egalitarian instincts, is that the *Vimalakīrti Sūtra* is extraordinary in its breadth of spirit and appeal. The ability to communicate effectively with the enormous variety of people is one skill that the author of this text, whoever it was, had in abundance. The sutra has been beloved by millions of Buddhists, from the most sophisticated philosophers to farm villagers who never tired of hearing stories of Vimalakirti's profundity. It communicates at all levels of sophistication, from colorful stories of divine beings and magnificent miracles to the cutting edges of Buddhist logic. The text collapses the rigid separation of philosophy and religion that is so puritanically strict in our own culture while demonstrating the limits and corruptions of all types of arrogant, dogmatic thinking.

Third, the *Vimalakīrti Sūtra* is at times truly hilarious. Throughout its dramatic episodes in the life of Vimalakirti, comedy and humor keep the weight of sophisticated philosophy from drowning its readers and hearers in the tedium of abstraction. The author makes fun of all rigidity, all dogmatic purity, and does so with ironic insight, even making a brilliant joke of the presumed intellectual/spiritual superiority of men over women. As a very early text committed to the enlargement of Buddhist thought and practice that was at that historic moment coming to be called the Mahayana, or "great vehicle," much of its humor emerges at the expense of earlier, "lesser vehicle" ways of imagining Buddhism.

These sectarian squabbles from early India need not detain us, however, nor, for our purposes, even interest us, especially since the best points made by early Mahayana thinking were quickly absorbed by all other types of Buddhism. What is being ridiculed in the *Vimalakīrti Sūtra* is rigidity and narrowness of vision—shortsightedness no matter whose it is. But comedy makes that point with daring precision, keeping Vimalakirti's story alive and vibrant for thousands of years. Prior to this time the human capacity for comic wit was largely missing in the serious and sometimes staid culture of Buddhism. After Vimalakirti, though, ironic humor becomes a liberating means of extending and deepening what it means to be a practicing Buddhist. As a corollary to this extension of the Buddhist dharma, the *Vimalakīrti Sūtra* has had an enormous influence on literature and the arts throughout East Asia.

Fourth, as a distinctive addition to the teachings of the Perfection of Wisdom sutras, the *Vimalakīrti Sūtra* helped provide the foundations for some of the most important developments in the later history of Buddhism. The breadth of appeal that the sutra had, its ability to overthrow hardened dichotomies like those between monastic and laity or between urbane philosophy and rural religion, and its adoption of humor as one of its many "skillful means" helped give birth to two of the most important kinds of Buddhism to appear in the subsequent history of Buddhism: Esoteric or Vajrayana Buddhism and Chan or Zen. My assessment is that this text belongs among the revolutionary spiritual documents of human history. However it should be evaluated, the *Vimalakīrti Sūtra* serves as a practical point of departure for our development of a Buddhist philosophy of life and our quest for concrete examples of skillful living.

The orientation of this book's focus on the *Vimalakīrti Sūtra* is contemporary rather than antiquarian, practical rather than scholarly. Through ongoing meditative dialogue with this sutra, it seeks to imagine the contours of a Buddhist philosophy of life suited to the diversity of twenty-first-century global citizens. Although occasional reflections on the origins and history of this sutra will emerge, this is not primarily an effort at historical reconstruction. However earlier Buddhists have used and understood this text through two millennia of multicultural Buddhist history, this interpretation, like its predecessors in their own settings, seeks current existential insight and models for contemporary ways of skillful living. In the same sense that the author of the sutra was not so much describing a person as developing an ideal for guidance in life, our Vimalakirti is an effort to visualize how on Buddhist grounds someone might live skillfully in our world, with insight, freedom, and compassion.

Quotations and citations from the *Vimalakīrti Sūtra* in this book are all from Robert Thurman's translation, *The Holy Teaching of Vimalakirti*, with page numbers from this translation noted in parentheses after each citation. In a very few cases I have made minor adjustments to that text based on consultation with other versions: the influential fifth-century Chinese translation by Kumarajiva, the excellent English translations from Kumarajiva's Chinese by John McRae and Burton Watson, the recent Thomas Cleary translation from the newly discovered Sanskrit version, and the erudite French translation from Tibetan by Etienne Lamotte. Although the *Vimalakīrti Sūtra* was somewhat less influential in the history of Tibetan Buddhism and elsewhere than it has been in China, Vietnam, Korea, and Japan, Robert Thurman's spiritually potent rendering of the sutra in English has already begun to change that. Buddhists from many different traditions have begun to see the insight and wisdom of this sutra emanating through Thurman's remarkable translation, which now stands alongside other historic versions of the sutra as a classic of spiritual literature.

1

The Path and the Buddha

At the Start of the Path

Standing at the trailhead of a well-known mountain hike, we find a large, wood-framed sign providing basic orientation to the path we are about to trek: cautions to be observed, rules to follow, a summary of the terrain to be traversed, information on what will be encountered along the way, and a rudimentary map as guide. Studying the map, we see a variety of alternative routes—sub-trails and side trails that separate and rejoin each other, some short and steep, others long and gradual. They offer several different ways to move in the same basic direction— all choices to be made as we make our way along the path.

Buddhism presents its teachings as just such a path, a route or set of routes through life toward a proposed destination with life-changing effects. Because this is a well-known path, traversed by many before us, we have some assurance that the trip is worth the effort—on some accounts, perhaps even extraordinary. At least others walking the path have said so. But for each traveler, the path will be explored anew, reimagined and reexperienced. Each journey along any path will be a unique experience, something personal created out of inherited opportunities and distinct points of departure. Hence, the Buddhist Sanskrit word for spiritual pursuit is *bhāvanā*, "to bring something into being," "to cultivate and create." No one can do this for us, even though there are helpful guides offering direction, instruction, and encouragement. Like the sign and map at the trailhead, guidance can be invaluable, most importantly at the outset but so too all along the way. But once we are on our way, the journey will be ours and ours alone.

The *Vimalakīrti Sūtra* opens like all other sutras, with the Buddha as our guide. His teachings—what he called the dharma—will give orientation to the path and present it in a way that inspires effort. In this text the teachings will be offered in a garden at a grand gathering

Living Skillfully. Dale S. Wright, Oxford University Press. © Oxford University Press 2021.
DOI: 10.1093/oso/9780197587355.003.0002

attended by many different kinds of people—monks and nuns of different schools of thought and practice, members of the lay community, the local youth group, even gods and goddesses. Before the Buddha's verbal teachings begin, a ceremony is staged, a grand pageant, culminating in a miraculous vision that focuses the minds of all attendees.

The Buddha's Miracle of Inclusivity

As the Buddha enters the luxurious, enclosed garden, there are literally thousands of observers eager to be in his presence. It's a warm, sunny day. Everyone takes a seat in expectation. The opening ceremony is to be performed by the local youth group. Five hundred strong, "each holding a precious parasol made of seven different kinds of jewels," they parade into the garden in splendid pageantry (12). One by one they bow to the Buddha in respect, circumambulate his seat seven times, and then, as an offering, place their parasols at his feet before withdrawing to take their seats. Then "suddenly by the miraculous power of the Buddha," the sutra says, the individual parasols "were transformed into a single precious canopy" covering not just all the guests in the garden but the entire land as far as anyone could imagine (12). Everyone gasps in astonishment and turns to the Buddha as the source of this spectacular display of power and generosity.

The Buddha doesn't explain the meaning of this miracle. The event speaks for itself. It was a hot day, as it almost invariably is in India. The parasols carried by members of the youth group provided shade and comfort for each of them individually. But that left everyone else out in the scorching sun without protection. The Buddha's miraculous intervention transforms all of the individual parasols into a single giant canopy sheltering everyone from the sun's intensity. Not content to accept the gift of individual parasols for his own comfort alone, the Buddha provides that comfort for everyone.

The audience senses that this generous offering of shade is a sign of the Mahayana, the Buddha's "great vehicle," not a distinct movement at that point in Buddhist history but a particularly demanding orientation within Buddhism. Although the *Vimalakīrti Sūtra* doesn't feature the word "Mahayana," it helped generate that view of Buddhism by cultivating the realization that any conception of Buddhism as a strictly individual spiritual quest is inadequate, even contradictory to the spirit of selfless awakening. The Buddha's non-verbal teaching in transforming individual umbrellas into an immense canopy for all is that we're all on the path of life together and that a fundamental part of the path entails unselfish concern for others. The sutra insists that the Buddhist path is inclusive, open to everyone equally. Therefore, the Buddha's first teaching in the *Vimalakīrti Sūtra* is that Buddhism is best understood as a path of transformation for whole communities, everyone included. The dharma is an open invitation.

Experiencing the Buddha Field

Then as soon as the canopy of shelter was in place, the Buddha extends the scope of the miraculous. Suddenly, by the power of the Buddha's mind, everyone in attendance gets to see the world as the Buddha sees it. Vision opens, extending out to encompass everything in all directions. No one had experienced such a magnificent expansion of mental capacity before. Attendees gasp in astonishment. After this brief glimpse of enlightened awareness, the Buddha withdraws the magic and everyone returns to their previous state of mind, but now energized with a sense that awareness of a far greater scope is possible. The sutra says that the entire crowd was "ecstatic," "enraptured," "astonished," and "filled with awe and pleasure" (12). After a poem of praise for this magnificent experience is recited, the visitors, now wide awake with expectation, have a chance to ask questions and to hear the Buddha teach the dharma.

A member of the youth group gets to ask the first question on behalf of the others. Naturally everyone wants to know what just happened. What was that enormous expansion of awareness and how did he do that? They want the Buddha "to explain to them the bodhisattva's purification of the buddha-field" (15). Bodhisattvas are Buddhists who serve the "maha-yana," the "great vehicle" traveling toward enlightenment that is expansive enough for everyone to get on board. The bodhisattvas' service gets under way with a vow to do something that at the starting point no one could possibly do. They vow to engage in transformative practices that will enable them to care as much about the well-being of all other people as they do about themselves. They vow to seek a depth of compassion and commitment to equality that stands far out beyond them as an ideal yet to be attained. And they vow to spend the rest of their lives working toward a revolutionary awakening of human spirit.

The Buddha explains. The bodhisattva's "buddha-field" is a sense of community and a sphere of influence, small or large, that extends as far as a person's wisdom and compassion make possible. The buddha-field that everyone in attendance got to witness briefly through the mind of the Buddha was enormous, encompassing literally everyone and everything. For others, it is a field of aspiration, an arena of transformative practice for those intent upon learning how to live differently. The Buddha offers several measures of that difference. First are the "six perfections": how to live generously, justly, tolerantly, energetically, mindfully, and wisely on behalf of all living beings (16). The Buddha then offers the "four immeasurables" as another standard of bodhisattva practice: to "live by love, compassion, joy, and impartiality" (17). His response to this initial question goes on to outline briefly several of the Buddhist teachings that the sutra will provide.

Bodhicitta: The Thought of Enlightenment

What the Buddha's answer to the youth group's question provided was an element of the Buddhist path that would get them started and guide them along the entire path of practice. This is a "thought of enlightenment" (*bodhicitta*), an always developing conception, aspiration, and desire of the highest order. It is the "mind of enlightenment," a guiding vision that makes it possible to engage in transformative practice. When this thought or aspiration takes hold in someone's mind, everything begins to change. What once seemed important fades into the background, gradually replaced by higher-order values that are to be deepened over time or replaced by even more comprehensive ideals. A thought of enlightenment is the big picture, a wider, long-term view of human possibility. It is an aspiration that can be consulted at any time to give direction to daily activities and to stir the energy of disciplined effort. For bodhisattvas, this wider view encompasses concern for the health and well-being of everyone, including the health of the overall culture that is being absorbed by everyone at all times without their even being aware of it.

Once developed, a thought of enlightenment is more than an abstract thought, more than one concept among others. When effective it becomes a driving aspiration, a desire that sheds light on all other desires. It is a thought that takes the position of what matters most—the ultimate concern guiding all other concerns. It inspires passionate, at times even erotic, striving. That description may sound un-Buddhist. Buddhists are well known to teach detachment from passionate desires based on the Buddha's realization that out-of-control desire is the root of suffering. But a finer distinction is important here. What the Buddha saw at the root of human suffering was *taṇhā*, best translated as "thirst," "craving," "attachment."

Taṇhā is compulsive grasping, desires that we haven't chosen but that have nonetheless invaded our mental landscape to the detriment of our health. An effective thought of enlightenment is an overarching desire, one that sets the standard in terms of which all other desires can be evaluated. An authentic thought of enlightenment provides a vision of life that makes it possible to detach from compulsive desires that can now, in view of *bodhicitta*, be seen as unskillful and unhealthy. The sutra calls this "the joy of extending enlightenment" (38), extending it by assessing desires as each comes under the scope of a powerful awareness of what is optimally possible for each of us as human beings.

Detachment, then, is the Buddhist response to unchosen, impulsive desires, and to desires that are harmful to oneself or others. But the point of detachment isn't learning not to care. It isn't the stark, lifeless effort to eliminate all desires and intentions. That form of tranquility more closely resembles death. It is learning what best to care about and how to care in a way that is maximally beneficial. Skillfully chosen desires are fundamentally distinct from obsessive, reactive ones. A great deal of meditative self-scrutiny in Buddhism goes into reducing or eliminating compulsive desires and into cultivating desires intentionally chosen for enlightened reasons. To the extent that desire, wanting, willing, and striving are closely linked together, desire is to be cultivated and shaped rather than eliminated.

A mature, well-developed thought of enlightenment is the result of a great deal of deliberation on what is truly worth desiring. What ideally should I want? Given who I am, what should I strive to attain, aside from what I just happen to want? That crucial question drives the development of *bodhicitta*, a thought of enlightenment. Unchosen desires are aimless, often pointless, whereas desires guided by a thought of enlightenment align with a guiding vision. The mental role that *bodhicitta* plays for a Buddhist is that of a standard or measure in terms of which all other desires can be evaluated for their contribution to the health of individuals and communities. An active thought of enlightenment provides guidance and direction in life and serves as a source of inspiration for energetic effort and transformative action.

So when the Buddha responds to the youths' question about the vision of reality that they had personally witnessed just moments before, he directs them to "the magnificence of the conception of the spirit of enlightenment," to *bodhicitta* (16). That's the place to begin. He says it entails "a field of positive thought," "high resolve," and "virtuous application" (16). A thought of enlightenment initiates a path of practice. It starts a lifelong process of transformation that enables skillful living at greater and greater levels of maturity based on visionary understanding that is more and more comprehensive through practices that delve deeper and deeper into the wellsprings of life.

Living in the World

The sutra has the Buddha continue to teach, now by leading a dialogue with distinguished guests in the garden that day. One of them, Śāriputra, a famous early disciple of the Buddha, expresses his dismay with this incurable world of pain and suffering. He says, "As for me, I see this great earth, with its highs and lows, its thorns, its precipices, its peaks, and its abysses, as if it were entirely filled with ordure" (18). Ordure is feces, human or animal excrement. Śāriputra's view is that this is a shitty world, an unredeemable world, and that his hopes are better placed on nirvana, an alternative abode of invulnerability and enduring bliss. Another garden guest then steps forward to question the assumptions underlying Śāriputra's complaint about the world.

He suggests that the "highs and lows" Śāriputra describes might be highs and lows in his own mind rather than features of the world. If the world seems like it's full of crap, as Śāriputra has said, the speaker recommends that we examine our minds and assess the point of view from which that seems to be so (18).

Without saying a word, the Buddha then rejoins the dialogue with another miraculous intervention. When he touches his big toe to the ground, once again everyone in attendance briefly sees the world as the Buddha sees it. It's gorgeous, all dimensions complexly interwoven and magnificent beyond belief—nothing smelly about it. The Buddha then repeats the basic idea: everyone always evaluates the world "according to their own degrees of mental purity" (19). What we experience and how much we understand depends on the clarity and depth of our mental state. Once we get this insight, he explains, the path of mind cultivation begins. Lacking a thought of enlightenment to inspire and guide the cultivation of mind, we will experience this world as a place of impurity and dis-ease. But it need not be that way, and the Buddha vows to teach everyone how to undertake that change. As these teachings were being discussed, the sutra says, some people in the garden were "liberated from their mental defilements, attaining a state of non-grasping" (19).

The fact that early Mahayana sutras repeatedly make this same critical point must mean that at least some Buddhists at that time had come to think of nirvana as so exalted a state that it couldn't possibly be located in this world of woe. Several early descriptions of this state of being did describe it in somewhat otherworldly terms—perfect peace and bliss, beyond our imaginations, unconditioned, and permanent. Or at least it had come to seem so superior to life in this world that it was simply assumed to be elsewhere, in spite of the many sutras that make it very clear that nirvana is a transformed mental presence right here where we are. So Mahayana texts repeat a motto-like formula: nirvana is *samsara*. Nirvana is this very world in which we currently live, experienced differently. It is a state of mental clarity in the midst of the life we're living, not a departure from it. There is nowhere else to go.

This same point is made a little later in the sutra when a group of women ask, "How should we live in the abode of Mara?" (38). Mara was the Indian mythological figure of the devil, and this world is the abode of Mara, just as it is also the abode of the Buddha and nirvana. We dwell in this one world according to the degree to which our minds have been transformed through a variety of meditative practices and life experiences. On this particular occasion, the sutra's response names the practice of generosity as one way to live in a mental state of nirvana while occupying the abode of Mara. Generosity is a state of mind that is open and gracious, and giving is an act that sets us free of our slavish self-absorption. When we engage in these selfless practices the world looks less like Mara's abode and more like the Buddha's vision that everyone got to sample.

What is it about living in the "abode of Mara" that tempts us to devalue the life we have by spending our time daydreaming of a different kind of life in another world? Our always recurring suffering, no doubt: the difficulty of living, the pain we experience, the troubles that never seem to go away, the rapid change and confusion—these lure us into imaginary excursions. In the throes of pain and suffering, and in the fear of them, we dream of a condition of perfect invulnerability where suffering isn't even possible. When we are mentally transported to another world, the life we currently live is belittled, sometimes reduced to being no more than a stepping-stone to a heavenly afterworld of absolute peace and tranquility. Things in heaven are unchanging, unconditioned, eternal, and perfect, whereas our current world is condemned as changing, conditioned, transitory, and flawed. In heaven there is no struggle, no effort at all is required. This daydream is a recurring temptation whenever the difficulties of life become overbearing. It offers a permanent vacation—from life as it is.

The Buddhist philosophy of life that we draw from the *Vimalakīrti Sūtra* advises against allowing ourselves to demean our lives with otherworldly fantasies. The sutra offers tactics that can be employed to reorient our lives in relation to suffering in order to remain focused on the issues at hand. One approach includes meditations to develop the realization that although difficulty and suffering are inevitable, they are parts of life that work in tandem with joy and elation. We can't have either without its opposite. This simple recognition and acceptance help to enable some degree of relaxation in relation to pain and hardship. Although troubles press upon us with great intensity, that will change. Whatever comes will also go. Whatever intensifies will diminish. Seeing this, even when pain is upon us, can allow us to let go of our stiff resistance, the tensing of muscles and the mental reaction of tight inflexibility.

It is possible to learn to do this, and when we do, we discover that rigid resistance to hardship and pain is in fact an additional source of pain. This is part of the "state of non-grasping" that Vimalakirti teaches over and over. It is also what the Buddha referred to as shooting second and third arrows at ourselves after being hit by a first arrow from some troubling part of the world. The Buddha proposes that we examine our compulsive and fearful reactions to pain and injury when they occur in order to identify the ways that we do in fact make it worse. Reactions are often so emotionally laden that, even in retrospect, we can't recognize and identify them with clarity. Our fear of hardship and pain is often so great that we turn away without ever examining our own contribution to the agony we experience. Lacking this awareness and without a "thought of enlightenment" sufficiently developed to empower a clear vision of further possibility, we confine ourselves to the "abode of Mara."

Who Is the Buddha?

The Buddha first appears in the *Vimalakīrti Sūtra* as a teacher who wields miraculous transhuman powers. Before speaking even one word in the garden that day, he instantly transformed small umbrellas into a giant canopy and thrilled the large crowd by enabling a religious vision of the vast scope and intricacy of the cosmos. This divine image of the Buddha is, of course, quite different from that found in the earliest sutras, in which the Buddha is a very human teacher. Although there would surely have been reverence for the Buddha among the early disciples, the predominant attitude shown in the early sutras is respect and admiration for their teacher as the original source of the dharma. This Buddha is wise and compassionate but still thoroughly human. By the time Mahayana sutras like the *Vimalakīrti* were being written, however, several centuries of enhanced storytelling about the Buddha and other famous religious figures had gradually, perhaps imperceptibly, upgraded finite human events into legends of the miraculous.

The *Vimalakīrti Sūtra*'s image of the Buddha shares many characteristics with other sutras composed around the beginning of the Common Era. Although the Buddha makes his appearance as an extraordinary and awakened person who has come to the garden that day to teach, his powers occasionally take on a transhuman character. In spite of these imagined powers, however, the Buddha remains a teacher and a guide throughout the sutra, not a savior. The Buddha is not credited with having created the world in which they live, nor is he its overlord. He simply works within the given reality to help people understand what is at stake in living healthy, awakened human lives. As the sutra says, "He serves as a bridge and a ladder for all people" (64), a bridge to the "other shore" of awakening and a ladder to ascend to a higher level of awareness. The miracles we read about in Mahayana sutras were considered skillful teaching techniques, an iridescent sign that Buddhism or this sutra had the power to bring about a substantial transformation in the quality of lived experience—a miraculous alteration in the way life could be lived. We should therefore attribute these miraculous events not to the Buddha as a historical figure but to the storytellers who employed them to create inspiring, transformative narratives that would be read, recited, and revered in many cultures for over two millennia.

The wisdom that the Buddha teaches does not come as a gift of divine grace. It must be earned through the discipline of practicing the dharma. The Buddha is presented as offering instruction, guidance, even occasional visions to help practitioners focus resolve. But ultimately each person is challenged to face the task of living on their own. The Buddha doesn't do that for us. Aside from encouragement and instruction, images of the Buddha don't have him intervening in the choices that each person has to make individually. His role is that of a healing teacher, a guide along one or another of the available paths that people would aspire to traverse on their own.

The sutra mentions one exception to this, however, which it offers without elaborating or explaining. What do you do to help when someone just can't manage on their own, when someone is completely overwhelmed by life and has no power left to begin movement out of this dire situation? What do you do for someone whose suffering is no longer educative, someone who is simply pushed further and further down by the undertow of destructive choices? What could you say to someone whose only recourse appears to be total despair, to give up on life? The sutra offers this: someone "who is terrified by fear of life should resort to the magnanimity of the Buddha" (57). Although no further explanation is offered, the implication is that worship of the Buddha, prayer, and petition are available practices, possible sources of enablement for those who have nothing left on their own.

When all resources have been exhausted, the sutra says, you can still turn to the Buddha's magnanimity for support and acceptance. Although the sutra was written to inspire meditative discipline and ardent practice, no disdain is shown for those whose situation in life renders them unable to engage in these disciplines or to take responsibility for their condition in life. Even though the sutra's overall position is non-theistic, it is not atheistic in our modern sense of a disdainful criticism of the idea of religious grace. Dismissive condescension of this kind just doesn't come up in the long history of Buddhism. When only prayer remains, that practice of appealing to the magnanimity of the Buddha summons the sacred power of graceful transformation and uplift.

As a teacher, then, the *Vimalakīrti Sūtra*'s Buddha is focused on the human condition and on how our lives are shaped by the quality of response we make to the realities of life that we all face. No redemption from this life is offered because life is not an evil condition from which redemption is needed. The ideal is not freedom from this life of difficulty, or even freedom from uncertainty, from having to make decisions and live with the consequences of our choices. We are at all times vulnerable to the difficulties of finite human existence because that is the kind of life we have—and there isn't another one to which we can transfer. What the Buddha claims, though, is that redemption from deluded responses to living this life is both humanly possible and profoundly transformative. This redemption requires turning toward the realities of life rather than away from them in fear and loathing. It requires an even greater commitment to life in the world than we have managed before.

What makes this transformation possible is an awareness within each of us, however vague and deeply buried, of an aspect of our nature that is even more fundamental than our suffering: a beauty and a kind of wonder that make rising above our suffering possible. From the perspective of this awareness, the real miracle is our being here at all, our living as we do in this world just as it is. We get a glimpse of how miraculous this life is whenever we experience something so beautiful that it bowls us over, or when we momentarily feel a quality of love so powerful that it brings us to tears. Suffering may be unbelievably harsh, but we just keep on living empowered by something at the heart of life that confirms it all—even the suffering. On this basis, bodhisattvas resolve not to be diverted by an escapist wish for another kind of life that is without choice or vulnerability, but rather to experience an awakening or rebirth in the midst of this life just as it is. Setting all fantasies aside, bodhisattvas commit to a quest for wisdom and compassion that will transform the way we collectively inhabit this world. Getting to that deeper sense of possibility is the beginning of the path, a point at the trailhead where a thought or aspiration for enlightenment takes hold of us and begins to alter how we live.

2

The Bodhisattva Ideal

The Life of Vimalakirti

Following a traditional formula for Buddhist sutras, the *Vimalakīrti Sūtra* opens by describing the setting in which the Buddha will teach and then begins teaching by articulating several important Buddhist principles. The second chapter, however, moves in an entirely different and unusual direction. It introduces another character who replaces the Buddha as the primary teacher. The central character in the story is Vimalakirti, a Buddhist layperson residing in "the great city of Vaiśālī," an ancient urban complex that the Buddha did in fact visit during his lifetime. Although Vaiśālī was a real place, it is unclear whether Vimalakirti was an actual person living there or not. For our purposes and for the purposes of the sutra, that doesn't matter. Whether the story is idealizing a real person or describing an imagined one, the point of the second chapter and the sutra as a whole is to plant the mental seeds of a new Buddhist ideal—that of an ordinary citizen who is both fully enlightened and fully engaged in a vibrant and complex urban world.

What Vimalakirti demonstrates in every aspect of his life is the ability to excel at the most sophisticated teachings and practices of Buddhist monastic culture while simultaneously living a very worldly life. By picturing this conjunction of presumed opposites in the life of its central character, the sutra suggests a possibility for Buddhism that no one had previously imagined. It claims boldly that the highest and most refined achievements of Buddhism are in fact open to anyone regardless of their vocation in life. Even though neither the *Vimalakīrti Sūtra* nor the newly emerging Mahayana movement meant to abandon the monastic ideal of early Buddhism, and even though that monastic preference continued for many centuries of Buddhist history in India and elsewhere, an extraordinary change was occurring in the composition and dissemination of this text.

Living Skillfully. Dale S. Wright, Oxford University Press. © Oxford University Press 2021.
DOI: 10.1093/oso/9780197587355.003.0003

This historic shift in ideals indicates to us that the concept and image of the highest human aspiration in Buddhism, the "thought of enlightenment," had been effectively enlarged, and those of us today who don't live monastic lives but who participate in Buddhist practices can consider ourselves to be among the beneficiaries of this expansion. Given that historic importance and its relevance for our time, it will be well worth our meditating on the character of Vimalakirti in some detail while asking ourselves what that development might suggest about our own efforts to envision a contemporary philosophy of life on Buddhist grounds. So we will inquire: How is Vimalakirti's enlightenment presented in the sutra? Who was he, what was he like, what did he do, what was he thought to have achieved, and what does the sutra say about how he came to be regarded by others in his community?

In English translation the strictly biographical portion of the second chapter is a full two pages in length. Aside from stories of the Buddha's life that were probably being written just prior to this sutra, the *Vimalakīrti Sūtra* gives the most detailed and concrete account we have of the life of a prominent Buddhist at this early point in Buddhist history. We assume Vimalakirti's story to be a fictional rather than historical account, but to a great extent so was the accumulating story of the Buddha's life. The author of this sutra was clearly engaged in an effort to envision the best possible ways to live a Buddhist life, whether as a layperson or as a monk or nun.

The chapter begins by making its primary point: Vimalakirti was a person living in the city of Vaiśālī; he was not a monk, but he was nonetheless profoundly awakened. It says: "He had penetrated the profound way of the dharma. He was liberated through the transcendence of wisdom" (20). Going further, it claims that Vimalakirti "lived with the deportment of a Buddha," and that he "was praised, honored, and commended by all the Buddhas" (20).

Vimalakirti's Skill

In addition to valorizing Vimalakirti's "realization" of the dharma, the author of the sutra praises his skill as a teacher of the dharma and places that teaching task in the overall setting of the Mahayana, the bodhisattva's vow to seek the liberation of all living beings. Vimalakirti has a lot of work to do. In order to be effective in his vow to extend awakened insight to everyone, what will be needed, the sutra asserts, is *upāya*. *Upāya*, often translated as "skillful means," or in this sutra translation as "skill in liberative technique," just might be the most important theme in the *Vimalakīrti Sūtra*. It is featured at the forefront of the Vimalakirti biography.

When the sutra praises his skill as a teacher of the dharma, that praise goes beyond what had already been said about Vimalakirti's understanding and internalization of the dharma. To teach skillfully he would certainly need to have achieved a profound realization. But skillful communication, the transmission of authentic insight or wisdom, takes more than that. It requires a comprehensive understanding of the varieties of people who will be taught, their different backgrounds, capacities, and styles of learning. So the sutra says: "Having integrated his realization with skill in liberative technique, Vimalakirti was expert in knowing the thoughts and actions of living beings. Knowing the strength or weakness of their faculties, and being gifted with unrivaled eloquence, he taught the dharma appropriately to each" (20).

Vimalakirti is pictured in solidarity with ordinary people. He truly understands them because he is one of them. He sees how they differ as unique individuals. He understands what motivates each of them into action, why they do what they do both when their actions are effective and when they are self-destructive. He senses the "strengths and weaknesses of their faculties" (20) and takes that fully into account in his efforts to enlighten them. Where he sees a serious problem with anger or resentment or passivity, he shapes the dharma to address that. If the issue is fear or anxiety, that becomes the liberating edge of his words and actions. That's what the sutra means in saying that Vimalakirti "taught the dharma appropriately to each" (20). While the dharma encompasses general principles (impermanence, dependent arising, four truths, the eightfold path, etc.), aligning these principles with the particular circumstances of individual lives is understood to be a further and more refined dimension of wisdom. That is the function of *upāya*, the "skillful means" that Vimalakirti had cultivated.

Thus, the sutra says that Vimalakirti "integrated his realization with skill in liberative technique" (20). That act of integration is crucial because it enables the most comprehensive vision of the dharma to penetrate down into the smallest detail of actual life. Through this integration, the overarching values of the dharma are actualized in each unique situation to create the transformative difference that is sought. In this respect the sutra implies that when the profound wisdom of insight or realization is integrated with the concreteness of skillful *upāya*, the result is wiser, worldlier wisdom. We might call it "effective wisdom" or, as Aristotle called something quite like it, "practical wisdom." So, in describing the lead character of the sutra, the author makes a major point of emphasizing the integration of profound wisdom with the exactitude of effective skill not in an ethereal or abstract realm but right here in our world of concrete issues.

Six Dimensions of Self-overcoming

With that overview in place the sutra then turns to some specifics of Vimalakirti's personal practice as a Buddhist. The first item of interest is Vimalakirti's practice of the six *pāramitās*, often translated as the "six perfections." These are the six focal points for self-sculpting that together were taken to be a comprehensive account of what enlightenment is. An enlightened person is generous, moral, tolerant, energetic, meditative, and wise. Each of these characteristics requires extensive cultivation (*bhāvanā*). Each must be literally "brought into being" out of seeds, roots, or potential that is already there. Therefore, Vimalakirti's ongoing practice included meditations designed to cultivate each of these traits: generosity, morality, tolerance, energy, meditation, and wisdom.

Although the theme of the six perfections comes up dozens of times in the sutra for various purposes, here is how the second chapter describes Vimalakirti's engagement with them: "His wealth was inexhaustible for the purpose of sustaining the poor and the helpless. He observed a pure morality in order to protect the immoral. He maintained tolerance and self-control in order to reconcile beings who were angry, cruel, violent, and brutal. He blazed with energy in order to inspire people who were lazy. He maintained concentration, mindfulness, and meditation in order to sustain the mentally troubled. He attained decisive wisdom in order to support those who had little understanding" (20).

The focus in this particular reference to the *pāramitās* is not so much on the actual practice of each "perfection" as it is on the purpose or motive for pursuing them. Why spend so much time and effort engaged in these difficult practices of self-transformation? What purpose or intention guides the practice? Here is his answer for each of the six:

- *Generosity.* Although Vimalakirti was magnificently wealthy, he spent that wealth not for his own pleasures and purposes but for "the purpose of sustaining the poor and the helpless" (20). The bodhisattva vow is to strive toward caring as much about others as you already do about yourself, and if Vimalakirti and his family are just fine while others are suffering, then the purpose of his riches becomes care for the poor and those who for whatever reason are experiencing great difficulty. He vows to be generous not because that is a good thing for him to be, which of course it is, but because others and the society as a whole will benefit from his assistance. Both are true, but Vimalakirti's expressed intention highlights the latter.

- *Morality.* Vimalakirti is represented as observing a very high level of moral conduct, not in order to lord it over those who are unable to do that but "in order to protect the immoral" (20). Why do the "immoral" need protection? Because the impact of their own deeds is devastating. They haven't learned that grabbing and pushing their way through life undermines their effort to live a healthy and satisfying life. They haven't understood that morality is the most essential form of protection for themselves and for others, not something they can avoid or only pretend to do so that they can focus on their own protections and benefits. Vimalakirti therefore seeks to be their protector by teaching them how to live morally. He lives his life as a model of moral excellence and dedicates himself to the well-being of others by teaching them the power of morality as the most effective form of protection for themselves and for the community as a whole.

- *Tolerance.* Vimalakirti practices tolerance, patience, and self-control not just in order to dwell in the equanimity of inner peace but "in order to reconcile beings who were angry, cruel, violent, and brutal" (20). Of course, engaging in these practices of tolerance did mean that Vimalakirti maintained profound equanimity. But that inner calm was seen as a gift that he could give to others who had no idea how to live in balance and harmony with themselves or others. Vimalakirti sacrificed some of his own peace to cool the fires of anger and hatred in others. So although it is hard to imagine a peaceful person wanting to spend time with people who were "angry, cruel, violent, and brutal," that was Vimalakirti's vow and his practice.

- *Energy.* Vimalakirti "blazed with energy," not the energy of self-assertion and competitive advantage but the compassionate energy of unity and cooperation. Energy of this kind is infectious. To be around a generator of joyful, loving energy is to be swept up in that energy and to have some portion of it seep into oneself. As we'll soon see, Vimalakirti was everywhere—in the schools, in the housing areas, in government, at sporting events, hanging out downtown, and more. He was a powerplant of irresistible energy that was on offer to everyone. His vow was to extend the discipline and the elation of energized life to everyone.

- *Meditation.* Vimalakirti "maintained concentration, mindfulness, and meditation in order to sustain the mentally troubled" (20). That's all of us. We all live in our own degrees and versions of mental incapacity, unable to concentrate for long, unable to stay on track with our goals, unable to make healthy choices, unable to get out from under the self-absorption and delusion that constrict our vision. Vimalakirti meditates not in order to rise above our mental immaturity, nor to avoid society's small-mindedness, but as a generator of mindfulness on our behalf. Just hearing about someone with that level of presence wakes us up. It shows us our own possibilities as well as our current limits. It shows us how we might live in greater awareness.

- *Wisdom.* Vimalakirti's practice of wisdom encompasses all of his other practices, and its aim is the fulfillment of his vow. He gives generously in order to enlighten others wisely and skillfully.

He practices morality, tolerance, energy, and meditation for the same reason—to fulfill his vow to help the rest of us live with vision and integrity. From inner resources of profound selflessness, Vimalakirti's wisdom is offered to those of us who have little in-depth understanding of life, those of us who don't realize how shallow our encounter with life really is. Vimalakirti seeks to wake us up, to put us on a path of freedom from our self-imposed slavery, and to show us possibilities for our lives that so far we've been unable to imagine. Wisdom is the key to the freedom of enlightenment.

The six perfections lay out the full scope of bodhisattva practice, and the account of them in the sutra's character sketch shows us their ultimate aim—awakening from the confinement of self-absorption to an open life of wisdom and compassion. Although we all begin our transformative practice, if we begin at all, focused entirely on all the good it will do for us as individuals, the long-term effect of these practices is to loosen that inevitable self-absorption and help us to see that liberation is not so much for the self as it is from the self. Awakening entails self-overcoming, and for Vimalakirti the six *pāramitās* are the basic elements of that ideal transformation.

Reconciling Opposites

Vimalakirti was unprecedented as a character type in Buddhism. Not only had there never been anyone like him, no one had even imagined this combination of personal traits to be possible. Vimalakirti represents a new way of living as a Buddhist. The third paragraph in his biography accentuates the unexpected nature of his persona. The key word in every sentence is "yet" or "but." These conjunctions accentuate the contrast between two seemingly irreconcilable opposites. The pattern goes like this: Vimalakirti lived in this worldly fashion, *yet* he also did what no one living that way would have done. He undermined people's expectations. If you do X, then you can't possibly be Y, or at least that was the assumption until the image of Vimalakirti was created. He is presented as a person who reconciles apparent opposites and enlarges awareness of what is possible. Here are some of the contrasting features that Vimalakirti held within the enormous scope of his life:

- "He wore the white clothes of the layman, *yet* lived impeccably like a religious devotee" (20). This first sentence puts the primary issue on the table. Either you live the life of a layperson or you live a monastic life—one or the other. That was the standard assumption. Yet Vimalakirti is pictured as a layperson who at least in certain respects lives like a monk. The next sentence clarifies the contrast.

- "He lived at home, *but* remained aloof from the realm of desire" (20). The assumption was that if you live in a family or social setting rather than in monastic circumstances, you couldn't possibly live free of the temptations and desires that drive laypeople and define their lives. Yet, we are told, Vimalakirti did. His discipline and mindfulness afforded him the freedom to choose which desires he would pursue and to simply ignore others.

- "He had a son, a wife, and female attendants, *yet* always maintained continence." Continence implies restraint, the monastic capacity to hold back from sexual inclinations. Since Vimalakirti is married and has a son, we assume that continence here means sexual restraint appropriate to his particular family status. The point is that unlike monks and nuns, Vimalakirti didn't have to withdraw from social contacts that might have been sexually provocative in order to maintain the depth of his meditative focus. He could maintain conviction and integrity in any setting, unprovoked by the provocative.

- "He appeared to be surrounded by servants, *yet* lived in solitude" (20–21). Vimalakirti lived in a busy household, a wealthy home that employed a staff of assistants. The "solitude" stressed here is the isolation of monks and nuns who dwell in tranquil monastic retreats. But Vimalakirti's solitude is a state of mind rather than a living arrangement. It didn't matter whether he was in meditative retreat, in his busy household, or in the city; his focus, his concentration, and the depth of his mindfulness were always in

effect. The sutra describes a capacity to remain in this contemplative state of mind while engaged in worldly activity.

- "He seemed to eat and drink, *yet* always took nourishment from
the taste of meditation" (21). Can you be a meditative person
while living in a world of sumptuous food and drink, without
being overwhelmed by craving? It hadn't seemed so before. But
as the sutra suggests, Vimalakirti did. Based on the discipline of
mental practice, self-indulgence was no longer a destructive tendency for him. His desires had been redirected and placed in the
service of his vow as a bodhisattva.

- "He made his appearance at the fields of sports and in the casinos,
but his aim was always to mature those people who were attached
to games and gambling" (21). Sports gambling and the nightlife of
casinos were considered the opposite of contemplative existence,
just as they are today. If you spend time in those contexts you are
vulnerable to corruption. Monks and nuns would have been absolutely forbidden to enter such venues and were exposed to the
possibility of expulsion from the monastic community if they did.
But Vimalakirti is pictured as perfectly able to visit these places of
shallow mentality without corrupting effects. He could help the
gamblers and idlers see the folly of their ways without being con-
descending and morally rigid, and without succumbing to their
weaknesses.

- "He understood mundane worldly practices, *yet* always took
pleasure in the delights of the dharma" (21). Monks and nuns are
said to "renounce the world." They give up all "mundane worldly
practices" that sustain laypeople. Yet Vimalakirti is imagined as
fully engrossed in these worldly practices while at the same time
engaged in a contemplative existence that elevates him out of
mundane states of mind. For him, the highest insight functions
to illuminate the smallest details of everyday life. Another point is
noticeable here. Seldom did Buddhists talk about taking "pleasure
in the delights of the dharma." Pleasure is what the ordinary
people sought, while the dharma was thought to entail a renunciation of pleasure. Pleasure and dharma just didn't go together—
until Vimalakirti.

Everything about these passages would have been unexpected, out of the ordinary, contrary to the common sense of the time and perhaps ours as well. Vimalakirti broke molds in all aspects of his life. He blurred standard distinctions and reconciled apparent oppositions, becoming a new model of Buddhist awakening. He practiced wise contemplative living right in the midst of ordinary life.

Full, Unprecedented Inclusivity

While monks and nuns were advised to seek out good spiritual friends and to spend their time with people who would help advance their quest for enlightenment, Vimalakirti was imagined to have offered his time and attention to anyone who might benefit from them. The sutra makes this point at great length:

- "He mixed in all crowds, yet was respected as foremost of all" (21). Maybe it was *because* Vimalakirti was able to mix in all crowds that he would be universally respected. The effort to "mix in all crowds," which, honestly, none of us really manages to do, was for Vimalakirti an obvious implication of his bodhisattva vow. You can't help people with whom you don't converse, people you don't really know. And if they don't know you, they will be more than skeptical about your offer to "help."
- "To demonstrate the evils of desire, he even entered the brothels. To establish drunkards in correct mindfulness, he entered all the cabarets" (21). The point here is clearly that Vimalakirti spent considerable time with people previously shunned by good Buddhists. These people are not good influences. Their destructive behaviors have karmic effects not just on them but on the whole society. That's the reason for Vimalakirti's concern for them, the point of spending time with them. His compassionate engagement with them is intended to help them recognize the destructive seeds that they have been sowing and to help them get out from under that negative impact. Who benefits from this spirit of inclusivity? All of us.

- "In order to be in harmony with people, he associated with elders, with those of middle age, and with the young, yet always spoke in harmony with the dharma" (21). Harmonizing with people requires that you speak their language, that you talk about issues that really do concern them and do so in ways that really get to the heart of the matter from their perspectives. Different generations think and speak differently and crossing those cultural barriers takes wisdom and empathetic rapport. And we all know how difficult it is to make this cross-generational contact without violating or ignoring our values.

- "To train living beings, he would appear at crossroads and on street corners, and to protect them he participated in government" (21). Spending time out in the world rather than in meditation retreat, Vimalakirti cultivated proximity to all of the people of his city. Attaining mutual understanding, they trusted him to represent them in government. Rather than argue for the political advantage of his own social group, as most politicians clearly do, Vimalakirti saw his role as protecting all of the people from the myopia and greed of political partisanship.

- "To develop the children, he visited all the schools" (21). The schools are where the seeds of future enlightenment are to be planted, where minds are open, malleable, and eager for understanding. While the elders are mostly set in their mental ways, and while the middle-aged folks are busy scratching out a living, the children can be remarkably flexible of mind. They are often able to envision ways of being that are fundamentally different and occasionally better than the customs and habits of their families and communities. Vimalakirti was right to focus here. No one else would have thought to do so. Let us imagine Vimalakirti the educator not as a stern, grim disciplinarian but as someone who enjoys life in such a way that the children want to be with him and want to learn. Just by being around Vimalakirti they learn to "take pleasure in being consciously aware" (83).

- "He was compatible with ordinary people because he appreciated the excellence of ordinary merits" (21). Although we don't really know what the author of the sutra had in mind here, we can imagine how we might want to fill in the blanks. Picture Vimalakirti taking an interest in the knowledge of the farmers, expressing admiration for how their intuitions are in harmony with the seasons, with the soil, and with the organic world that sustains us. Imagine him praising the potter for the skillful means etched into her hands and mind. Picture him truly appreciating the knowledge that it takes to cook, to sew, to build, to raise children, and expressing clear appreciation for these invaluable contributions. Do aristocrats ever do that? Vimalakirti did.

Taking Care of Business

The sutra pictures Vimalakirti as a respected businessperson, as a property owner and landlord, and as a government official. And he's rich, very rich. We were already told that "his wealth was inexhaustible for the purpose of sustaining the poor" (20), and now it is clear that Vimalakirti has numerous sources of wealth creation. The point of telling us about all of these ventures, however, is to demonstrate how someone could be involved in that world of profiteering while at the same time carrying out the bodhisattva's vow of compassion. We might assume that no one could do both. Vimalakirti is presented as the bodhisattva who proves that this contradiction between the creation of wealth and caring for others is not inevitable, that it is possible to engage in business motivated not by greed and personal gain but by humanitarian convictions. Here are some of the sutra's pointers in this direction:

- "He engaged in all sorts of businesses, yet had no interest in profit or possessions" (21). We should read this to mean "no interest in profit or possessions" *for himself.* If you run a business, you can do so on behalf of yourself, your employees, your customers, your community, or any combination of these. But running it successfully assumes some interest in profit, even if you are not among those who will profit. The ideal is to use the profit from a business enterprise for humanitarian purposes, directing that money toward the public good. The bodhisattva's practice is aimed not at the suppression of desire but at its reorientation to a purpose larger than individual gain and personal pleasure. Bodhisattva business owners would purposefully cultivate a desire to advance the common good through skillful entrepreneurial means.

- "He was honored as the businessman among businessmen because he demonstrated the priority of the dharma" (21). Whatever the author may have meant here, we can't possibly concur if this "priority" is sought for Buddhism over some other religious group as a claim of religious exclusivity. But if dharma means "the truth," or "the principle of wisdom and compassion," or "the most admirable values conceivable," whatever they are, and if that is the way that Vimalakirti ran his businesses, then it is easy to see why he would be "honored as the businessman among businessmen." Good businesspeople are honorable in the sense of "honest," but to give priority to higher values over personal profit, that is exceptional.

- "He was honored as the landlord among landlords because he renounced the aggressiveness of ownership" (21). The "aggressiveness" that we associate with landlords is quite simply the self-absorbed greed that compels property owners to take excessive advantage of their privileged position. Can you renounce the aggressiveness of ownership without renouncing ownership? Indeed you can, and we can all sense the difference between landlords who lord it over their tenants by squeezing every issue to their financial advantage and those intentionally practicing justice, generosity, and understanding in their maintenance of the landlord/tenant relationship.

- "He was honored as the aristocrat among aristocrats because he suppressed pride, vanity, and arrogance" (21). Those who find themselves in aristocratic, privileged positions quite naturally exude "pride, vanity, and arrogance." They view their privilege as somehow earned, deserved, and rightfully theirs. Focused on taking full advantage of their superior position, they fail to see the arrogance in their behavior, arrogance that is obvious to everyone else. Vimalakirti is pictured as noble in the ways that he practiced his nobility, noble in understanding the ultimately undeserving character of his position in life. He is noble in the primary position that he has given to his vow—equality to all.

- "He was honored as the official among officials because he regulated the functions of government according to the dharma" (21). Here again, we read "dharma" as the open ideals of truth and compassionate principle. Vimalakirti served as a government servant on behalf of the people. What mattered was justice, universal well-being, the health of the society as a whole. That is the dharma, his governing ideal. Whereas for most of us the opportunity to hold a position in government is a chance to better our own careers and lives, for Vimalakirti that was far from the point. He entered government as an extension of his vow to care deeply about the well-being of the whole community and to awaken everyone to their own deepest potential.

The image of Vimalakirti that has been sketched out in the sutra and that we've tried to recreate here presents an ideal that we cannot imagine fulfilled. Vimalakirti was everywhere helping everyone and always in a profound state of mindfulness. No one could do all this while maintaining integrity and sanity. But ideals are not descriptions of achieved realities. They are mental images of aims and intentions to guide our everyday practice even though we cannot yet live up to them. Vimalakirti's aim was to live in accordance with his vow of compassion for all living beings, and he is described as doing that in every conceivable context. So if we're businesspeople, we see what it would mean to be principled in our pursuit of profit. If we're landlords, we get a model of a relationship to tenants that is fair and respectful. If we're Buddhist meditators who shun loud, complicated urban settings, we are given an image of someone who maintains mindfulness even in the most troubling, complex circumstances.

In Sickness and in Health

When the biographical description of Vimalakirti's character comes to an end with praise for his "skill in liberative technique"—his *upāya*—Vimalakirti's teachings begin. This is the substance of the sutra, but its uncanny brilliance is the way it communicates the teachings of Vimalakirti through dozens of captivating stories, each one an episode in the life of this lay bodhisattva. The sutra's author doesn't just admire the virtue of skillful means. Whoever wrote this sutra had that skill in abundance. The sutra's teachings are sophisticated, complex, sometimes difficult, but the stories that do the teaching are riveting, and their ennobling effect has made this sutra one of the greatest teaching tools in the history of Buddhism.

The teachings begin: "At this time, out of this very skill in liberative technique, Vimalakirti manifested himself as if sick. To inquire after his health, the king, the officials, the lords, the youths, the aristocrats, the householders, the businessmen, the townfolk, the countryfolk, and thousands of other living beings came forth from the great city of Vaiśālī and called on the invalid. When they arrived, Vimalakirti taught them the dharma" (22).

Vimalakirti pretends to be sick. Actually, he is sick. As long as human beings live in unhealthy, deluded, and self-destructive habits of mind, Vimalakirti shares our illness and works with us from within that sickness in pursuit of healthy, skillful living for everyone. The bodhisattva vow is to be there with us and for us, not above us or beyond us. As long as some of us are suffering, we all suffer. This is true of all of us, but there is a crucial difference— Vimalakirti is imagined to share our suffering in so profoundly conscious a way that it shapes his every move. This understanding of the matter also provides him with a cure. He says: "What is the elimination of this sickness? It is the elimination of egoism and possessiveness. What is the elimination of egoism and possessiveness? It is the freedom from dualism" (45).

Dualism is an isolating sense of separation, a feeling of being fully on one's own in life, unconnected to others, to the natural world, to the whole of reality. Overcoming dualism is the cure for suffering. Therefore, Vimalakirti teaches: "Recognizing in one's own suffering the infinite suffering of these living beings, the bodhisattva correctly contemplates these living beings and resolves to cure all sickness. As for these living beings, there is nothing to be applied, and there is nothing to be removed; one has only to teach them the dharma for them to realize the basis from which sicknesses arise" (45–46).

Thus, Vimalakirti uses his personal sickness as a skillful means of teaching all of us the larger meaning of sickness and health for humanity. The third chapter continues this same theme. The setup is this. Vimalakirti is at home on his sickbed teaching the locals. The Buddha, some distance away, nevertheless reads Vimalakirti's mind and smiles at the chance to have him teach others as well. So the Buddha asks one of his favorite disciples, Śāriputra, to go visit Vimalakirti to check up on his health. Śāriputra responds by declining the invitation. He says: "I am indeed reluctant to go ask Vimalakirti about his illness. Why? I remember one day when I was sitting at the foot of a tree absorbed in contemplation..." (24). Śāriputra goes on to tell a story about his encounter with Vimalakirti, who shows up to raise questions about the character of his meditation practice. Śāriputra is amazed by the wisdom of Vimalakirti, a mere layperson. So he explains to the Buddha that he was unable to reply to Vimalakirti's teachings on that occasion, hence his reluctance to go repeat that embarrassing encounter.

What had Vimalakirti said to Śāriputra that rendered him silent? He had questioned Śāriputra's monastic withdrawal from the world. He had explained that meditation isn't primarily a means of retreating from the world but rather a way to engage it directly, a way to see it more clearly and to enable more skillful involvement in it. A truly meditative life seeks to be more thoroughly exposed to the world rather than sealed off from it. So Vimalakirti recommends another way to become "absorbed in contemplation." He says: "You should absorb yourself in contemplation in such a way that you can manifest the nature of an ordinary person without abandoning your cultivated spiritual nature" (24). The common sense of the time held that it was one or the other, certainly not both. If you have cultivated your spiritual nature you can no longer be an ordinary worldly person engaged in the affairs of the day, and if you are involved in that kind of worldly life then you aren't living a spiritual life. Vimalakirti questions this assumption and lives a life that demonstrates how both are simultaneously possible. Indeed, he suggests that a life of retreat from the world might indicate a lack of understanding, the mistaken view that awakening could ever be a solitary, individual possession.

Vimalakirti also questions whether an enlightened life is one of complete dispassion, a life detached from the emotions that keep the world in motion. He tells Śāriputra: "You should absorb yourself in contemplation in such a way that you are released in liberation without abandoning the passions that are the province of the world" (24). To abandon all of the passions of life is to abandon life. Emotions or feelings are a fundamental part of what it is to be alive, an essential dimension of human life. Emotion is one of the five components of life for Buddhists (*skandhas*), such that a truly human life includes a full range of emotions as an essential element. For Vimalakirti, the point of monastic detachment is to undermine the destructive emotions. These are feelings that arise from dualistic isolation and self-absorption. They include such ruinous states as anger, hatred, resentment, jealousy, and many others that are well known to us for their unhealthy and destructive effects.

But there are also constructive emotions, feelings that empower and sustain life. Joy, compassion, awe and wonder, love and kindness—these are emotional, even passionate states of mind that an authentic life gracefully encompasses. The point of bodhisattva practice is to cultivate a life that is physically, mentally, and spiritually passionate in its encounter with all dimensions of human experience. Vimalakirti vows to take in the pain of all living beings—to really feel it—without succumbing to the fear, resentment, self-pity, and anger that typically accompany it. Vimalakirti challenges Śāriputra and all of his readers to consider the nature of detachment more thoroughly.

Then, among other disciples, the Buddha turns to his son, Rāhula, who is also a Buddhist monk, asking him to go check up on Vimalakirti. Rāhula gives the same response: "I am indeed reluctant to go to Vimalakirti to inquire about his illness" (31). Rāhula then tells the story of his encounter with Vimalakirti's uncanny wisdom. He says that he was teaching a group of young men "the benefits and virtues of renouncing the world" when Vimalakirti shows up to raise some difficult questions. Vimalakirti explains that "renunciation" isn't about individual "virtues and benefits" at all, and that it isn't about abandoning the world. The point is that everyone already desires "virtues and benefits." That's the problem because the benefit they seek tends to be for themselves alone. True renunciation, Vimalakirti teaches, is a "bridge over the swamp of desire, without grasping, and free of the habits of 'I' and 'mine'" (32). Without self-absorption, without clinging to the "benefits" of possessions or security, Vimalakirti teaches how to live in mindful awareness and love.

Embracing rather than renouncing the world, Vimalakirti goes on to teach Rāhula and his young students how to be "truly renunciate" without literally abandoning the world. True renunciation, he explains, is an internal act of transformation. It lets go of self-centered grasping and attachment. "It disciplines one's own mind and protects the minds of others" (32). To renounce active life in the world rather than one's own grasping and clinging is to forgo the chance to awaken. "To be a human being is very precious," he says (32). Don't renounce your opportunity to live it completely. So Vimalakirti explains: "Young men, you should cultivate yourselves intensively to conceive the spirit of unexcelled, perfect enlightenment. That in itself will be your renunciation and high ordination!" (32). Riveted on a visionary "thought of enlightenment," bodhisattvas freely release other subordinate concerns by encompassing all things at a higher level of compassionate awareness. In ardent view of *bodhicitta*, that "letting go" is easy, hardly the deprivation that renunciation had seemed to be. For Vimalakirti, that expansive transformation is the true meaning of "renunciation" and the very point of Buddhist "ordination."

3

Self-overcoming

Vimalakirti is pictured in the sutra as an ardent practitioner of the six *pāramitās*—six dimensions of character that are open to cultivation at an advanced level of enhancement. *Pāramitā* here indicates the aspiration for human excellence at its highest level. More specifically, *pāramitā* means "going beyond," beyond oneself, beyond what has previously been possible or conceivable, overcoming the limitations of one's current way of living. Hence the "six *pāramitās*" practiced by Vimalakirti are most often translated as the "six perfections" or "six transcendences." The *pāramitās* are a central theme in the *Vimalakīrti Sūtra*. They are praised and recommended in almost every chapter.

Buddhists frequently specify that what is transcended—what a bodhisattva goes beyond—is the self. That is to say that all six dimensions of human excellence—generosity, morality, tolerance, energy, meditation, and wisdom—are thought to be practiced at the level of *pāramitā* when they are performed without the kinds of self-interest that typically motivate and define our actions. Vimalakirti is described as being generous, for example, with no concern for how his generosity might benefit himself. He provides assistance to others not because others might be generous to him in return, nor because he will be praised, respected, or admired as a result, nor to clear his conscience, nor even to enlighten himself. He does it simply because someone needs his help. His acts are motivated by something beyond the kinds of self-concern that drive the rest of us. In that sense the *pāramitās* are disciplines of self-overcoming.

Self-overcoming Through Generosity

The *Vimalakīrti Sūtra* names generosity as an essential feature of Buddhist enlightenment. The Buddha and enlightened bodhisattvas

Living Skillfully. Dale S. Wright, Oxford University Press. © Oxford University Press 2021.
DOI: 10.1093/oso/9780197587355.003.0004

are pictured as generous above all else. They give themselves—
their time, their resources, their wisdom, and their compassionate
attention—to all living beings. As with other human virtues, though,
their generosity is not innate. It "arises dependent" upon specific
causes and conditions that need to be cultivated. Bodhisattvas' ability
to give is the result of a discipline of mental training. They have trained
their minds to respond to others in a spirit of open generosity by visu-
alizing the plight of suffering beings and all of the ways that they might
help alleviate their suffering. Meditating repeatedly on possible acts
of giving, they strive to internalize deep feelings of generosity so that
when real opportunities for giving appear, generosity comes forth naturally and spontaneously.

In that sense, then, rigorous, long-term training in the *pāramitā*
of generosity is not meant to culminate in the stiff disciplinarian who
suppresses instincts of self-interest in order to fulfill a moral obligation
to give. Quite the opposite, in fact, since the *Vimalakīrti Sūtra* repeatedly links generosity to joy. You cannot create joy by joyless means.
When another bodhisattva asks Vimalakirti, "What is the great joy
of the bodhisattva?," he responds: "To be joyful and without regret in
giving" (57). He calls it "the love that is giving" and describes it as "free
of the tight fist" of self-absorption (57). Furthermore, Vimalakirti says
that "the *pāramitā* of generosity is consummated in peacefulness and
self-discipline" (39). Self-discipline that is relaxed and peaceful comes
naturally and is not forced. As it matures, therefore, it seems less and
less like discipline at all. As in the movements of great athletes, we
see intense effort without struggle, effort that is poised and balanced
rather than flailing awkwardly against the grain of life. As an outcome
of long-term training, discipline reaches its apex in tandem with joy
and ease.

But if joy and ease in giving are the eventual outcome of the
bodhisattva's background of training, this is not where any of us begin.
We begin where we are, in habits of self-aggrandizement and self-
protection that shape the small acts of giving that we do manage. This
self-enclosed posture is the point of departure for the first *pāramitā*,
self-overcoming through training in the refined arts of generosity.

Any act of giving places the donor's self-understanding on display,
and we can all intuitively distinguish between giving that is heavily

self-promoting and selfless acts of generosity. Even more to the point, we can all see these differences in ourselves, in our own acts of giving, if, that is, we have the courage to look closely. What motivates us to give up something that we want ourselves—our money, our time? We naturally ask ourselves, what would we gain that would make us want to give anything like that up? Perhaps it's the possibility that people will "return the favor" and be generous to us so that, in effect, very little would have been lost. Or maybe we give because people will respect us, admire us, praise us.

Or perhaps giving enables self-respect; it makes us feel good about ourselves, or clears our conscience. By being generous we would actually *be* good people because that's what good people do. We might also be motivated to give because in the long run generous acts would help us in the afterlife, or secure a better rebirth, or reap auspicious karma. The motives for giving are numerous, each rationale showing us something basic about who we really are behind the act of giving.

Questions about motives for giving don't typically have either/or answers. Motives are almost always multiple and mixed. Most of us do care about the cause or person to whom we have given. We give in order to be helpful, but at the same time we care about the prospects of praise and reward for our acts of generosity. We can see this most clearly when we make certain that others know about our gifts, when we time or stage our acts of giving so that we get full credit for the generosity of our gift or deed. To what extent do we seek to have our name associated with the outcome of our gifts and to be remembered in perpetuity for our generosity? Or are there occasions when we just give generously and then let it go with no tangible recognition at all? It is in these various senses that all acts of giving show the particular shape of the donor's own self-understanding. To anyone who is mindfully observant, all of our acts reveal who we currently are.

It's easy to see these self-serving weaknesses in people's acts of giving. But should we criticize and discourage acts of giving that are motivated by some form of self-concern? Usually not. Acts of self-promotional generosity are nonetheless still acts of giving. In most cases that is better than no giving at all. They may very well be a step in the right direction, one step toward developing more virtuous motives for giving. Even acts of generosity motivated by hopes for praise may yield substantial benefit to the one in need or to the one who happens to be in a position to give. After all, when we first learn to give, whether as children or as adults, the motivation of self-concern is crucial. We won't give without reasons, and at some level our reasons are all about what is good for us.

We learn to give for self-centered reasons at first because those are the only kinds of reasons we have. We just are self-concerned—all of us initially. From this point of departure it is perfectly natural to give for ulterior motives, motives that promise some attractive reward for us as givers, even if that is only the praise or self-congratulation that we might receive. Still, based on that immature motivation, we manage to give what we would otherwise keep for ourselves. And in doing so, what we discover is that, against all expectations, it is liberating to give. We feel a sense of freedom, exhilaration—a feeling that on future occasions we may hope to duplicate.

What is the basis of this freedom and why is it so satisfying? Vimalakirti says that in an authentic moment of giving we are "free of the habits of 'I' and 'mine'" (32), that the feeling derives from being "without grasping," "without attachment" (32), and "free of the habitual notion of possession" (25). He says further that in a generous act we are "joyful and without regret" because the weight of our "selves" has been momentarily lifted. That sense of exhilarating selflessness is what generates "the great joy of the bodhisattva" (57). In being able to give, we feel some degree of elation, a sense of being lifted up out of ourselves into an experience of liberation that is buoyant and joyful, even if momentary.

As the practice of giving deepens over time, as these mental exercises that develop the inner capacity to care about others begin to seep into our minds and habits, we become able to give for fewer and fewer ulterior motives, less out of concern for self-benefit and more out of real care for someone else's well-being. Working past deeply embedded habits of self-absorption is extremely difficult, precisely because these habits are so much a part of our cumulative character, the result of literally millions of unconscious acts generated out of concern for our own safety and well-being. For this reason, the *Vimalakīrti Sūtra* insists that practices of generosity must be accompanied by skillfully honed wisdom and that we should always be on the lookout for false forms of generosity. The sutra calls some of these deficient forms of generosity "sentimental compassion" (46), which is concern for others that hasn't been purified by life-altering insights into the impermanence and non-self-centered interdependence of all beings.

One bodhisattva in the sutra directs our attention to a limit on generosity that shows up at a very exalted level. He says that the practice of "generosity for the sake of attaining enlightenment is dualistic" (75). By this he means that giving in order to attain selfless enlightenment *yourself* is, ironically, still a form of generosity with ulterior motives and therefore cannot quite reach its goal of selflessness. It elevates you the generous donor above the needy recipient and in that sense doesn't fulfill the bodhisattva's vow to care just as much for others as you do about yourself. The sutra has another bodhisattva say that this "dualism is produced from obsession with self" (76), which arises out of misunderstandings about who we are and how we are related to others. This same bodhisattva goes on to say that "true understanding of self does not result in dualism" (76).

Bodhisattvas who embody a profound sense of non-duality or non-separation between themselves and others give quite naturally. And in so doing they "serve as a bridge and a ladder for all people" (64) to awaken to the freedom and joy of selflessness that true bodhisattvas demonstrate in every interaction. Cultivating insight into the ultimate selflessness of all reality, the bodhisattva sees clearly that all life is a gift, and that this realization liberates people from unnecessary confinement. On these grounds, Vimalakirti provides a comprehensive definition of the perfection of generosity. He says: "The giver who makes gifts to the lowliest poor of the city, considering them as worthy of offering as the Buddha himself, the giver who gives without any discrimination, impartially, with no expectation of reward, and with great love—this giver, I say, totally fulfills the *pāramitā* of generosity" (41). Such a person displays in her or his actions what "self-overcoming through generosity" means.

Self-overcoming Through Moral Development

The second *pāramitā* practiced by Vimalakirti is morality. The sutra tells us that he sought to overcome his own background of greed, hatred, and delusion by practicing "a pure morality" (20). Self-discipline of this kind was considered fundamental to Buddhist practice from the very beginning. The threefold division of the Buddhist path included morality, meditation, and wisdom. The Buddha had advised that among these three essential domains of practice, morality comes first, a prerequisite to any serious meditation or wisdom. Moral life meant a sensitivity toward others, justice in all relationships, and this required both mindfulness of one's own impact on others and the discipline of self-rule to initiate personal change.

At the most basic level this morality entails a strong commitment to five Buddhist precepts: to refrain from harming living beings, taking what has not been given, inappropriate sexual relations, false speech, and intoxicants leading to carelessness. More than simply prohibitions, these precepts were understood to be "paths of training," training not just to put an end to immoral acts and negative karma but gradually to transform the practitioner's mind and motivations. Developing moral sensitivity by overcoming earlier immature relations to other people, bodhisattvas sought to evoke profound self-overcoming.

After clearly affirming the basic principles of Buddhist morality, the *Vimalakīrti Sūtra* dwells on two more subtle points that were less frequently emphasized in the earlier tradition. The first of these is the problem of mental attachment to moral rules. Monks and nuns who follow the strict rules of monastic life—the Vinaya and the ten precepts—do so in order to overcome their numerous self-centered attachments in life. In order to redirect how their time is spent, they discipline themselves not to eat after noon, even though like everyone else they crave the comforts of food. And in order to redirect their mental focus and their energies, they eschew sexual engagement altogether, even though for most of them that goes against their instincts and inclinations. Through demanding disciplines of self-control like these, they overcome the kinds of personal habits to which we all become deeply attached. Using the Buddhist rules to enact that important transformation, however, exposes monks and nuns to another form of attachment—a rigid, invariant holding on to the rules themselves as a form of self-protection or self-congratulation.

This kind of "clinging" to the rules stands in the way of the development of a deeper moral consciousness in the same way that craving and attachment cloud our relations to everything else. Wherever rule-following becomes mechanical or simply guarding one's own moral standing, the deeper sensibilities and flexibility always present in profound human relationships fail to develop. The *Vimalakīrti Sūtra* tells a brief story that illustrates the problem. A goddess attending a gathering of Buddhists at Vimalakirti's house rejoices in the wisdom she has heard and gleefully showers the assembly with fragrant flowers. The light petals float gracefully by some of the guests but stick to the garments of the monks. Embarrassed to be strewn with color and fragrance because of their monastic vows to eschew adornment like jewelry or perfume, the monks shake frantically to separate themselves from the flowers.

When the goddess inquires about their frustrated efforts, the monks tell her that being adorned with flowers is simply not proper for them as monks due to their vows. The goddess smiles and explains. The reason the flowers cling so stubbornly to their bodies, she says, is the stubbornness of their mental clinging, the rigidity of the rules in their minds. The flowers float gently past the bodhisattvas who dwell in fearless equanimity and whose moral skill allows them to assess the situation at a deeper level. If the monks worked their minds through the constraint of the rules to that deeper level of morality, they wouldn't have to fret over the propriety of wearing flowers. Wear them, don't wear them—they'll be fine. People judge them, people don't judge them—they'll be fine. She says: "One who is without such thoughts is always proper" (59). The goddess then teaches the monks how not to be "intimidated by fear of the world" (59). She teaches letting be, a skill of balanced relaxation and equanimity.

The sutra teaches that, like everything else, the rules are "empty" of absolute, unconditional status. Like everything else, their validity came into being dependent upon certain conditions, and when those conditions change or differ, so might the applicability of the rules. The rules sometimes need to be reconsidered or modified over time as circumstances change. Clinging to the rules, holding on to them dogmatically, is a sign of misunderstanding. The moral rules are means, not ends, and when means and higher ends are in tension with each other, skilled bodhisattvas learn to practice the rules with appropriate sensitivity and flexibility. They still attend to the rules but now with skillful dexterity.

Rules are social conventions that generalize what would be good to do in situations of a certain kind. Although these rules are a convenient standard against which to judge the quality of our actions, the variety and uniqueness of moral situations require a fine-tuned sense of perception and judgment to determine when and how the rules apply to particular circumstances. Situations and people differ. The most appropriate actions are tailored to fit each unique situation with wisdom and compassion. Although the moral rules are helpful guidelines and should be given full scrutiny, a deeper responsibility to all living beings governed by wisdom and compassion may on occasion overrule the rules. Or as Vimalakirti puts it, the bodhisattva "who is interested in the Dharma is not interested in attachment to the Buddha, attachment to the Dharma, or attachment to the Sangha" (50). Moral wisdom enables letting go of all rigid clinging.

The second emphasis that the *Vimalakīrti Sūtra* brings to the issue of Buddhist morality has to do with sources of motivation—what is it that draws us toward moral action? We have seen that people are motivated to treat others fairly by a whole range of possible rewards—to be liked, to be admired, to be successful, and so on. The sutra describes Vimalakirti's motive for moral action in this way: "He observed a pure morality in order to protect the immoral" (20). Why did Vimalakirti practice the *pāramitā* of morality? To protect others, to help the rest of us engage in the art of skillful living. This simple sentence suggests a far deeper source of motivation than is generally thought to induce people to act with moral sensitivity.

Although that is his own source of motivation, Vimalakirti is pictured as extremely skillful at working with a broad range of people, people who are morally motivated in very different ways. Some people align their actions with the moral standards of their culture because that is the smart thing to do. Morally sanctioned acts are often the most effective way to attain their own ends. If you want your store to profit over the long run, you'd better not cheat your customers; if they realize you're cheating them, they will shop elsewhere. If you want to live happily in this neighborhood, you'd better not treat your neighbors with disrespect and disdain. Refraining from such behavior yields a better life for you.

At this basic level, morality is mostly about restraint—what you ought not to do. Thou shalt not kill, lie, cheat, discriminate, pollute, and so on. You will be rewarded if you are able to restrain yourself from such acts and punished if you do not. Buddhist teachers have traditionally warned that failure to restrain yourself from precept violations will produce bad karma and lead to a diminished rebirth. All moral teachings of this sort target people whose primary or only motivation is what they get or don't get as a result of their actions. If the rewards are attractive enough, people will do what it takes to get them.

Vimalakirti understands that level of motivation and isn't dismissive of it. He works with people at whatever level of understanding their words and actions show. He does so, however, not just to get them to obey the moral rules but to help them undergo a basic change in orientation. He hopes to help them work through their "inferior aspirations" toward the higher goals of an authentic morality. Rather than being motivated by what they want and don't want—by motivational traces of greed and hatred, craving and rejection—he hopes they can be motivated by the possibility of becoming a different kind of person, a selfless source of wisdom and compassion, someone who joins in the creation of a better, more respectful kind of community.

Beyond basic moral restraints, there are many positive, healthy goals to which people aspire. At this level we can aspire to be a good person, someone who has earned the trust and respect of other people. Leading a moral life in order to become an admirable person, we internalize the moral code as a dimension of our inner character. Rewards for oneself are still the primary aspect of our motivations, but they now stand at a much higher level. A traditional Buddhist who lives a life serving others with kindness expects that this will accrue good karma and ensure a beneficial rebirth. These are all very good reasons to treat others as you would hope to be treated, even if they are still at least partially self-serving reasons.

Most of us will see our own motives described here, reasoning that makes sense to us. But the sutra attributes to Vimalakirti a very different set of motives. He lives an impeccable moral life not because the rewards it offers are so attractive or even because that's the kind of person he aspires to be. He lives morally on behalf of the rest of us who are currently unable to do that and suffer as a result.

Vimalakirti's morality, in other words, is less a function of self-concern than it is of concern for "all living beings." That difference changes everything. Vimalakirti's authentically moral actions are not best described as a form of restraint or self-discipline. He doesn't sacrifice what he would much rather do in order to be just to others. Justice comes naturally because that's what he wants. This effortless morality is based on a fundamental transformation in his identity, a thorough self-overcoming.

The sutra pictures Vimalakirti living his bodhisattva vow, that is, caring as much about the well-being of others as he does about his own. He lives selflessly, as though he has or is "no isolated self," because his sense of identity now encompasses his relations with others. The self/other dichotomy has been transformed in the *pāramitā* of morality. The boundaries that once defined his identity in opposition to others have been enlarged to include others. That is a significant dimension of what it means to live selflessly. Although Buddhist texts routinely refer to this as an experience of "no-self," it could just as easily be described as an expansion of the self, an enlargement empowered by a profound reverence for the whole of life. On this image of the bodhisattva, Vimalakirti requires no awkward self-discipline, no rerouting of intentions. He is pictured as motivated by the well-being of the whole community, by the totality of living beings. He seeks not his own separate well-being but the viability and integrity of life itself because he understands what we have yet to fully internalize—that the viability of life *is* our own viability.

Self-overcoming Through Tolerance

The *Vimalakīrti Sūtra* features tolerance as one of the most profound characteristics of awakened bodhisattvas. Descriptions of Vimalakirti focus over and over on the depth of his capacity for tolerance. But tolerance here means much more than we typically associate with that word. More than the tendency to tolerate differences among people, the concept is here closely linked to wisdom, to compassion, and to selflessness. The sutra says, for example, that "attainment of tolerance of the emptiness of things is the entrance into non-duality," and that the "*pāramitā* of tolerance is consummated through the principle of selflessness" (39). Let us ponder what these claims might mean.

The Sanskrit word *kṣānti*, frequently translated as "tolerance," means being "able to endure," "able to withstand," "unaffected by" situations in the world that would overwhelm and undermine the rest of us. It indicates a deep composure and strength of character that allow the bodhisattva to face enormous difficulties without collapsing under the pressures of fear and anxiety. This third *pāramitā* is often translated as "the perfection of patience," "endurance," or "persistence" because it encompasses the calm, composed strengths of imperturbability and resilience. Intentionally training in this inner strength over time, bodhisattvas build the capacity to face danger, suffering, and injustice, to resist being overwhelmed by negative emotions, and to remain composed under the stress of great difficulty and turmoil. In situations where others are unable to function coherently, the bodhisattva continues to work effectively toward helpful solutions.

Having trained in the power of tolerance, Vimalakirti is pictured as being beyond typical weaknesses of character. He doesn't lose focus when things get complicated or difficult. He is not overwhelmed by fear. He doesn't react with anger to verbal or physical abuse but maintains the ability to deal with these issues in skillful and effective ways. And no matter how tough things get, he doesn't set his values aside or fall into hopeless despair. Because of this, Vimalakirti is imagined to preserve his energies in order to make constructive advances toward useful and noble goals. Not retaliating out of hatred and anger, not overwhelmed by destructive temptations, he stays on course when others have given up or gone astray. He maintains self-control and presence of mind in order to make the best possible moves under what others experience as intolerable circumstances. Far from a form of passivity or weakness, Vimalakirti's tolerance is a remarkable manifestation of strength.

Buddhist teachings on the capacity for tolerance are related to the realization that human suffering is an inevitable factor in our lives and that everything depends on how we respond to the impact of pain, threats, and a whole range of difficulties. When we lack the preparation of thoughtful, disciplined training in how to face suffering, our instinctual habits of response will deepen the negative impact that suffering has on our lives. Our instincts in this respect are often destructive. We instinctively shoot second, third, and fourth "arrows" at ourselves, as the Buddha's parable made clear. We respond badly to fear, overindulge in emotions of loss, and fall into despairing surrender far too easily. Living skillfully requires that we work in advance to examine our response patterns under such pressures, and that we transform the counterproductive ways we face up to all the difficulties of life. And in this domain, the sutra gives us Vimalakirti as a model to consider.

The practice of tolerance asks us to learn to face fear and difficulty directly rather than to turn away from them in denial, flight, or fantasy. Doing this requires dealing with deep-seated physiological response mechanisms. When the going gets tough our heart rate escalates, our breathing becomes rapid and shallow, and our reflective functions lose composure and lucidity. Facing life's difficulties skillfully entails reversing some of these instinctual response systems. The practice requires learning to work *through* difficulty rather than around it, to acknowledge it consciously, name it, and examine it deliberately—to look at it directly, with eagerness to understand and with disciplined intention. This is the opposite of passive acquiescence. It calls for resolution out of previously developed sources of strength. Two forms of meditation are particularly effective here: "calming" meditation for composure and "visualization" meditation to anticipate and premeditate difficult situations.

In describing Vimalakirti's practice of tolerance, the sutra says that "he maintained tolerance and self-control in order to reconcile beings who were angry, cruel, violent, and brutal" (20). This passage connects the practice of tolerance to the bodhisattva vow—the vow to engage in disciplined practice not just on behalf of our own enlightenment but for everyone equally. But in the case of "beings who are angry, cruel, violent, and brutal," that is extremely difficult because most of our relations to others are contingent on how they treat us. We treat them with justice and compassion so long as they aren't violent and brutal to us. Vimalakirti's vow, however, is to treat them compassionately no matter how they treat him in return. His tolerance is not negotiated. It is unilateral, a principled and compassionate relation to others regardless of their response. This goes against our instincts, instincts that have been shaped by long-standing habits of self-protection, the concern for personal security.

Does this mean, then, that Vimalakirti would tolerate absolutely everything in the sense of doing nothing to stop cruel and destructive behavior? No. His tolerance is not indifference. Vimalakirti is pictured as caring deeply about everyone—those who are victims of cruelty and injustice and those who perpetrate these crimes. Tolerance of this kind is not moral neutrality; nor is it blank dispassion or passive inaction. On the contrary, it is an impassioned commitment to the highest standards of morality, going beyond morality to the higher justice of love. In response to cruelty, Vimalakirti's tolerance is a simple refusal to be drawn down into the anger and hatred of others; instead, he responds to their cruelty with composure, inclusivity, and carefully honed skill. Doing so means not just stopping the violence on this occasion but seeking to heal the anger and hatred that gave rise to injustice and cruelty in the first place.

Vimalakirti's stance of compassion and inclusion encompasses those who are "violent and brutal." It seeks to undermine postures of animosity by including even those enveloped in anger and hatred into the circle of *us*, those about whom we care. This larger vision of community takes account of the needs of everyone, even those whose violence has done great harm to that same community. Our instinctual posture of exclusion toward those among us who violate our peaceful coexistence serves to replicate their acts of violence by turning us against the perpetrators. True justice demands deep understanding, and neither self-righteous anger nor revenge can bring that about.

This is why the *Vimalakīrti Sūtra* links the *pāramitā* of tolerance to non-dualism and to a "love that is imperturbable" (56–57). When we act "non-dualistically," with a commitment to inclusion and open community, cycles of retaliation that breed more and more injustice in the name of justice can be brought to an end. Wise tolerance neither allows further acts of violence to occur nor places the violent person outside the community's circle of care and compassion.

The sutra says: "Dualism is produced from obsession with self, but true understanding of self does not result in dualism" (76). The criminal's dualism is blatant and extreme, expressing hatred for others in the community by violating them. But justice as revenge is also dualistic, even if provoked by the first act of duality. Both sides seek exclusion of the other. Dualism, the passage says, is "produced from obsession with self," "self" positioned in opposition to the other, even the self in acts of self-protection. Another equally revealing passage goes on to say: "The *pāramitā* of tolerance is consummated through the principle of selflessness" (39).

The highest form of tolerance, in other words, occurs when we act as though our own interests and selves are no more (and no less) important than others', when we extend the "we" to include them. But you can't act that way by just deciding to. There are reasons for our intolerance and our impatience that reach down into deep layers of mental habituation. Insight into the ultimate "selflessness" of all things, of all beings, is something that occurs through practice at an extraordinary level of openness and flexibility. Although we cannot make that insight occur, we can put ourselves into a position where it might conceivably come to us. For Vimalakirti, that openness can be cultivated by practicing "self-overcoming through the *pāramitā* of tolerance."

Self-overcoming Through Energetic Effort

The sutra says that Vimalakirti "blazed with energy" and that his "energy inspired people" (20). It teaches that balancing your life on the "seat of enlightenment," as Vimalakirti did, "releases energetic activities" (36). And as we've seen, far from being aloof and unavailable, Vimalakirti was everywhere in the city of Vaiśālī doing quite literally everything in the spirit of selfless joy. He saw through the inherent duality and religious defeatism in the world-negating conception of enlightenment that some Buddhists maintained. His energy was fully in the world, of the world, and for the world. Naturally, then, the sutra honoring him is extraordinary in the extent to which it affirms life in this very world and makes ironic fun of every religious aspiration or desire to be somewhere else. That level of this-worldly spiritedness or vitality is produced, we are told, by overcoming (going beyond) oneself through the practice of the fourth *pāramitā*, energy.

The word "energy" here translates the ancient Sanskrit word *vīrya*, which named the strength and courage of the warrior. As the concept evolved, it signified the exertion and energy necessary to make extraordinary accomplishments possible. Early sutras referred to the Buddha as a *vīra*, the hero whose spiritual achievements would transform the world. The perfection of this energy, then, is the highest level of striving, the power of unyielding commitment to the final goal of universal awakening. The "perfection of energy" encompasses all of the following: striving, effort, strength, vitality, commitment, courage, and confidence.

Vimalakirti is confident, *con fide*, literally "with faith," faith that, in spite of all of its suffering and negativity, life in the world is inherently good. Although the sutra never describes it, when you read it you can't help but see Vimalakirti's beaming smile and wholehearted laughter. He winks at us on almost every page. His wink shows us how demeaning our fear, apathy, and world-weariness are. He's having fun, while taking life much more seriously than we ever do. Imagining Vimalakirti blazing with energy excites us about being similarly empowered through spiritual practices of mindful discernment and self-transformation.

The most potent Buddhist tool for the cultivation of transformative energy is *bodhicitta*, the "thought of enlightenment." Although this initial image of a deeply authentic way to live begins as a concept, it gradually evolves into a heartfelt aspiration, a deep desire to break through the barriers of self-confinement and into a larger vision of human awareness and commitment. The thought of enlightenment inspires energy to engage in mindful disciplines of self-overcoming, and those begin and end in a set of practices that we have come to know as meditation.

Buddhist meditation begins with a focus on breathing, precisely the place where mind and body come together. Learning how to breathe consciously, we learn how to absorb energy intentionally. Although from our first gasp of breath onward in life, we breathe without paying attention, when we do begin to attend to it we experience how mindful breathing wakes us up, revitalizing body and mind with an infusion of oxygen. The practice of mindful respiration is closely correlated with the perfection of energy. The Buddhist reversal of mind/body dualism is conspicuous here. Mind and body are intertwined, ultimately inseparable, and that essential element of non-dualism comes to fruition in breathwork meditations just as it does in the related disciplines of yoga.

The relationship between energy and desire has been difficult for Buddhists to clarify. The early "noble truths" held desire in suspicion as the cause of suffering. Perhaps "thirst" or "craving" (*taṇhā*) differed from the larger domain of desire, but disentangling them had become a philosophical and practical problem. On the one hand, many desires limit our vision. They lure us off course, influencing us to rationalize and to distort the integrity of our ideals. Meditation practices were designed to curtail desires so that spiritual vision would not be clouded.

On the other hand, the author of the *Vimalakīrti Sūtra* appears to have seen that human lives lacking desire would lack all motivation. They would be "apathetic," lacking the pathos of energetic concentration that any awakening would surely require. Desires are the source of drive and aspiration in human life. They provide the energy for a whole range of human accomplishments, including the spiritual quest for awakening. *Bodhicitta*, the thought of enlightenment for all living beings, evolves in the minds of bodhisattvas to become the primal desire, the deepest source of energy.

The *Vimalakīrti Sūtra* seems to recognize these two sides of desire— desires that demean and destroy lives and desires that liberate them. So the sutra can say that Vimalakirti resided in a state of desirelessness while at the same time making the counterintuitive claim that the "very nature of desire . . . is itself liberation" (60). Bodhisattvas skilled in practices of mindfulness learn the art of evaluating desires, testing them against a thought of enlightenment. Immature, uncultivated desires that are incompatible with this higher vision are identified and subordinated to others that align with wisdom and compassion. The goal of this kind of meditative discipline, then, is not just the repression of desires but their reorientation. The point is greater and greater freedom from compulsion, freedom to choose among possible sources of motivation, among desires.

Similarly, energy is interwoven with human emotions. Emotions both contribute to and detract from any intention to wake up from a life of daydreaming. The early Buddhist suspicion of human emotions runs as one thread through the entire history of Buddhism. In fact, a common caricature of Buddhism emphasized an emotionless, dispassionate life of non-involvement. It is certainly true that when we are consumed by passions like anger and hatred, or blinded by resentment or greed, we lose all freedom of choice and tend to act in ways that we later regret. Suspicion in these situations is fully warranted. But Buddhists quickly became aware that other emotional states contribute to open awareness—love and compassion, of course, but also awe and wonder, joy, laughter, and more.

In order to make this constructive contribution to a comprehensive thought of enlightenment, however, emotions need to be shaped and educated through mindful introspection. The intentional development of emotions plays an important role in Buddhist meditation. Emotional intelligence—bringing our emotions to maturity—makes us far less vulnerable to destructive outbursts of passion and opens up the possibility of experiencing a level of positive empowerment not otherwise available. Realizing this, there is no reason to think of Buddhist enlightenment as devoid of emotional passion—forms of joy and ecstatic letting go that can make an entire life truly worth living.

No reason, then, for a dour caricature of Buddhist ideals in which the struggle against the grain of emotion takes precedence throughout the life of a joyless disciplinarian. The *pāramitā* of energy should be understood differently to enable a passionate, even erotic, striving that culminates in an effort that goes beyond one's own striving. This is what Vimalakirti calls "joy in the pleasures of the dharma" (37), a condition in which the boundaries of the self are broken through. You have broken through the boundaries of self when you experience what Buddhists call "sympathetic joy," the experience of someone else's joy as your own. Such joy has released all self-sufficiency and self-confinement in exchange for loving affirmation of life. For Vimalakirti, this is the heart of non-duality.

Not holding back in fear and reticence but living wholeheartedly as a result of emotional development, bodhisattvas are able to act in accord with themselves and others. Feelings and energies that are signified by the heart are joined in harmony with the mind and the will, and through that cooperation, liberation from self-destructive forces begins to take hold. These meditative results make possible the effortless action that we see in the great Zen masters and other Buddhists whose energies have been concentrated in extraordinary ways. Self-overcoming through the *pāramitā* of energy means going beyond the limiting conception of "my" energy, incorporating into one's life the realization that we are all interlinked with everything around us and that in the final analysis everything *is* energy. This is Vimalakirti's secret, precisely what empowers him to be energetically everywhere doing virtually everything with a radiant smile of equanimity and joy on his face.

4
Practicing Meditation

The *Vimalakīrti Sūtra* presents its leading character as a master of meditation, an active practitioner whose every move in life already shows the profoundly liberating effects of that practice. The sutra's author refers to a wide variety of meditation styles and orientations, including *śamatha* (mental calming), *vipassanā* (insight), *samāpatti* (absorption), *dhyāna* (contemplation), *samādhi* (concentration), *bhāvanā* (cultivation), yoga, and others. These contemplative practices are said to "generate fitness of mind" (36) for overcoming a long list of human weaknesses: mental agitation, inability to concentrate, aimlessness, sense of futility in life, depression, despair, self-absorption, aggression, self-aggrandizement, boredom, resentment, anger, greed, hatred, delusion, debilitating fear, sensual desire, self-loathing, and many more. Moreover, the effects of these meditative exercises are not limited to states of mind. They entail "disciplining body, speech and mind" (89), as the sutra puts it, picturing Vimalakirti to have attained extraordinary depth in these practices.

But recall that Vimalakirti is not a monk. He doesn't live in a monastic environment where every aspect of life is designed to facilitate meditation practice. So although a couple of times we read of Vimalakirti entering into the meditative state of *samādhi*, overwhelmingly we encounter him fully engaged in the world rather than stepping back out of it to meditate. As a bodhisattva who has vowed the awakening of all sentient beings, Vimalakirti has work to do. He is almost always teaching, even when it may not appear that he is. On the surface of things, he's a businessperson out doing business, but the way he conducts business shows that he is also teaching the dharma. He is a landlord overseeing his properties, a father and husband attending to the needs of his family, a government official debating the issues of the day, an aide working in the schools, and an ordinary citizen who

Living Skillfully. Dale S. Wright, Oxford University Press. © Oxford University Press 2021.
DOI: 10.1093/oso/9780197587355.003.0005

spends time in bars and casinos. But always, along with these other activities, he is teaching.

As we imagine Vimalakirti's complicated life of bodhisattva activity, we can't help but ask ourselves—when does he meditate? How does he ever have time? Given that extensive experience in meditation is considered essential to Buddhist awakening, and given that monastic life is specifically organized to facilitate and to deepen meditative experience, how is it possible that Vimalakirti's realization could be so much more comprehensive than that of the many monks he encounters, as the sutra makes a point of demonstrating from beginning to end?

One of the implications of this sutra is not only that ordinary lay life is an acceptable role for dedicated Buddhists but also that this form of life is well positioned for a range of practices inspired by the bodhisattva vow of wise, compassionate involvement in the world. Meditation is, after all, not an end in itself but, as the *Vimalakīrti Sūtra* says, a discipline that "generates fitness of body, speech, and mind" for an enlightened life of purposeful activity. If the contemplative practices of meditation are ultimately *for* active life, then long-term monastic retreat *from* active life might not be the best way to deepen its effects, at least not always or for everyone. As many of us know from firsthand experience, it is one thing to be profoundly mindful on a meditation retreat in the mountains and quite another to maintain that state of heightened awareness at the scene of a traffic accident, in the midst of a political argument, having just disappointed a loved one, in the market, or at work. From this point of view, the highest level of meditative skill isn't deep absorption into otherworldly trance but rather a focused state of steady awareness that functions effectively in the midst of life's constant movement and complexity. That down-to-earth function of meditation is one of the central themes of the *Vimalakīrti Sūtra*.

This crucial theme in the sutra goes beyond grappling with the problem of how to extend the results of meditation out into everyday life. It is more importantly an effort to make everyday life itself the venue for meditation practice. The most comprehensive word for meditation in the sutra and elsewhere in Indian Buddhism is *bhāvanā*, often translated as "developing," "cultivating," or "bringing into being." Consciously engaged in *bhāvanā*, we develop or cultivate "body, speech, and mind" by "bringing into being" greater awareness in all aspects of life. In this sense meditation encompasses a wide variety of ways to cultivate wisdom and compassion in the midst of life. For Vimalakirti, everything—every encounter, every problem, frustration, and issue—is an opportunity for practice. Learning to transform whatever comes up into a focal point for meditation allows Vimalakirti to bring the stillness of deep concentration into the always surging flow of everyday life. This broader image of meditation gives rise to a sense that meditation is much more than a specialized exercise done in solitude in a particular bodily posture.

Since all aspects of life are amenable to development by means of contemplative practice, meditation could be extended to encompass virtually everything we do. As this thought germinated in early Chan Buddhism in China, one of its central slogans emerged: "Everything is practice." Every thing, every where, and every when—conscious breathing, mindful self-awareness, concentrated attention on the matter at hand in view of *bodhicitta*, one's largest, most expansive intention, the thought and aspiration for universal awakening. Guided by this enlarged understanding of meditation, practice became less a special exercise performed in time out from ordinary life than an open condition of body, speech, and mind in which one dwells. Rather than one training activity among others, meditative practice infiltrates every moment of life.

In its effort to explore this reorientation of meditation practice, directing us back toward the world and away from trance-like states of mind that take practitioners out of the world, the *Vimalakīrti Sūtra* employs long-standing images of the middle way. Ideal states of practice are located between the mindless escapes of ordinary life and concentrated trances that escape the world in the other direction. So here is how Vimalakirti teaches the monk Śāriputra to practice the middle path of meditation:

> You should absorb yourself in concentration in such a way that you can manifest the nature of an ordinary person without abandoning your cultivated spiritual nature. You should absorb yourself in contemplation so that the mind neither settles within nor moves without toward external forms. . . . You should absorb

yourself in contemplation in such a way that you are released in liberation without abandoning the passions that are the province of the world. (24)

For many practitioners of meditation, "abandoning the passions" would have been the point of the practice. That's why the sutra describes Śāriputra's response as utter silence. He's incredulous, completely baffled by Vimalakirti's counterintuitive advice. But Vimalakirti isn't seeking an escape from the joys and sorrows of life—the passions. He wants to experience them fully along with everyone else but to do so in a way that is not imprisoned by them. He wants his practice of meditation to encompass all of life, including the emotions, to harness their energy toward a more open and liberated way of being in the world.

So when the sutra advises "taking pleasure in solitude [of meditation] without being attached to it," it takes another step toward bringing meditation back down into the world as a means of developing the capacity for skillful living. What needs to be developed? Well . . . everything: the way we experience our fears and anxieties, the way we communicate and commiserate with others, the way we work, eat, play, and suffer. Nothing falls outside the domain of the practice of awakening.

Meditation as Calming and Concentration

If nothing falls outside the scope of meditation practice, where should we begin? Although the insightful slogan "Begin anywhere" (Zen composer John Cage's advice) makes sense in view of what Vimalakirti seems to be saying and doing, that is not the advice we would likely have heard from him. Instead the tradition of Buddhist meditation, from the Buddha himself all the way through two and a half millennia of Buddhist history, maintains that respiratory awareness—mindfulness of breathing—is the place to begin.

The Buddha instructed his followers to dwell in concentration by means of mindfulness of breathing. Practitioners are to feel the physical sensations of breathing, concentrating fully on that single internal process: sensing the air enter the nose, feeling the abdomen expand

and contract with the flexing and release of the diaphragm. In order to facilitate concentration so that awareness doesn't wander off in other directions, instructors often advise counting each breath up to ten and then starting over, one through ten. Meditators are taught not to force or to reform this natural respiratory process but just to watch and feel—no analysis or effort to improve. Observe as our bodies do the rhythmic dance of breathing that they have done since their first moment of entrance into the world.

This simple exercise is excruciatingly difficult at first. But when the mind wanders off, as it invariably does, meditators gently return to the next breath and start all over again. Why is this particular exercise regarded as the point of departure for Buddhist meditation? Along with the steady pumping motion of the heart, the rhythmic back-and-forth movement of respiration is the inner cyclical motion of all mammalian life. These bodily cycles put us in touch with one of the most basic rhythms of organic life. It is our foundation, our grounding in biological reality. Absorbing oxygen through the lungs and into the body replenishes and soothes all other processes. The cyclic movement of the heart and lungs functioning in perfect coordination keeps everything else in motion. Not breathing—any restriction to the flow of oxygen—immediately begins to shut the whole organism down, mind and body. When first felt, it incites panic, fear at the most primal level. To be sensually aware of the movement of air in and out of our central chamber is to be attuned to the very foundation of our lives. It brings us into focus in the present moment.

As this practice develops and deepens, the link between breathing and mental awareness becomes more and more obvious. Nothing brings us into a state of concentration and enhanced awareness more than mindful breathing. Lacking enhanced awareness by way of conscious breathing, we fall into default patterns of mental wandering and agitation. We live minute to minute in an unfocused state of slavish distraction. Slavish because whatever comes to mind controls our consciousness beyond any choices we have made. Mindfulness of breathing is a concentration practice aimed directly at overcoming mental distraction. It functions to expand our capacity to focus and be attentive without being possessed by unchosen thoughts and emotions. Buddhists used the word *samādhi* to name an extraordinary state of concentration, no longer waylaid or imprisoned by the spin-ning cycles of unwanted mental images.

But "mindfulness of breathing" is simply a useful starting point for more extensive practices of "calming" and "concentration." These med-itation practices can take anything as their focal point—an object, a sound, a color, and so on. The point is simply to focus in a way that calms or clears anxious, repetitive cycles of emotion-laden thought, unhealthy cycles of worrying, planning, and fantasizing over which we have virtually no control. As concentration grows through prac-tice, these compulsions weaken and our minds begin to enter a calmer, freer mode of experience.

Vimalakirti is pictured in the sutra as a master of this deep interior freedom. When he enters into *samādhi*, great mental powers became available to him. These powers are symbolized in this sutra by miracles that Vimalakirti—like the Buddha—can bring to fruition. Without losing our focus to the details of these literary excursions, we can see the enormous respect that was accorded to anyone capable of that de-gree of mental concentration. This dimension of meditation, calming and concentration, is the foundation upon which all other types of mediation practice can build. We should picture Vimalakirti solidly grounded in this practice as he goes about his complicated life of full involvement in the community.

Meditation as the Cultivation of Insight

Vimalakirti's meditation practice focuses directly on the dharma, the Buddhist teachings, and on meditative techniques designed to weave these liberating insights into the deepest levels of "body, speech, and mind." The sutra is, in fact, a guided meditation through the dharma's central issues aimed at transformative insight, which is how it has been applied to practice throughout Buddhist history. It prescribes *vipassanā*, insight meditation, in a slightly modified Mahayana form. As in earlier traditions of insight meditation, the Mahayana practice focuses initially on the "three marks of existence," teachings about the impermanence and selflessness of all reality, and the ways those two factors give rise to human estrangement and suffering. As did earlier forms of insight meditation, Mahayana texts extend beyond the "three marks of existence" to encompass other key principles of the dharma, especially "dependent arising," the "emptiness" of all elements of reality, compassion, and, in the case of the *Vimalakīrti Sūtra*, the ultimate non-duality of vibrant, interdependent reality.

What is insight meditation and how does this type of meditation give rise to realizations that are transformative in the way the sutra suggests? Insight meditation entails "mindfulness of dharma"— remembering it, bringing it to mind, understanding it and its implications, then integrating it into the functional mentality of real life by experiencing it at levels of mind deeper than linear thought can go. Insights that go deep enough are integrated into all aspects of "body, speech, and mind." Lacking that level of integration, their effect is substantially diminished.

Does this meditation practice include or require the activity of thinking or is meditation located entirely in a non-conceptual domain of mind? There is a tendency among some modern teachers of meditation to maintain that authentic meditation and thinking are fundamentally different activities and that thought is an obstruction to this central Buddhist practice. Although there is an important element of truth to this idea, it turns out to be more misleading than helpful. Insight meditation begins in focused reflection on teachings about the three marks of existence. Their development as concepts in our minds is crucial. To begin, we hear or read what the sutras teach about the impermanence of all reality and then rigorously think those ideas through in order to understand them thoroughly. The Buddha emphasized active inquiry in this practice, real questioning that goes beyond simply memorizing ideas or accepting them on faith with his assurance. Clarity and depth of thoughtful discernment are essential. The early sutras insist that we must do this for ourselves in order to understand what Buddhism is about and to be transformed by this understanding.

The truth suggested by the effort to keep thought and meditation separate is that not all forms of meditation entail active reflection and that the kind of thinking that it does require is neither calculative nor scientific, nor in the final analysis objective. Insight meditation teaches existential inquiry, interior probing that from beginning to end has a direct bearing on all aspects of the meditator's existence. Insights that emerge in reflective meditation are not reducible to intellectual conclusions or conceptual outcomes. They are neither objective nor impersonal in that they affect all aspects of a person's existence. In translating our version of the *Vimalakīrti Sūtra*, Robert Thurman calls it "transcendental analysis." *Vipassanā* is frequently defined as meditative insight into the true nature of reality. But "insight" here concerns not just one of the five components (*skandhas*) of human existence— thinking—but all of them. Insight is understood in thought, activated in altered perceptions, felt in the emotions, shaped by the will in transformed motivation, and realigned in self-consciousness as a new way of being in the world.

Insight meditation begins with contemplation of the first of "three marks of existence"—the truth that nothing in our experience remains the same over time. Impermanence (*anitya*) is the starting point of the path. This is also the first realization that the *Vimalakīrti Sūtra* describes when it has the people gathered around the Buddha exclaim in amazed realization that "all constructed things are impermanent" (19). It's interesting that this first insight is always presented in negative form—things are "im-permanent," not permanent—rather than positively, "everything changes." There is a widely prevalent religious and philosophical assumption east and west that the most important things, those of supreme value, must be permanent. The absolute, the unconditioned, the eternal, unchanging perfect reality stands apart from our ordinary experience as a dream-like ideal, something beyond this world of transience that can be trusted always to be exactly what it is now.

As is well known, the Buddha argued against this widespread assumption in Indian metaphysics. The world of change and complexity right before our eyes is the spiritual world, he proclaimed, and there is no other world besides this one. Neither Brahman, the pure unconditioned absolute, nor Atman, the eternal self of Indian religion, has a role to play in Buddhism. Nor does God as First Cause and Creator or the permanent heavenly world over which God presides. Instead, Buddhists begin with a recognition that the changing, conditioned world in which we live is as real as anything would ever need to be.

Insight meditation involves pondering not just changes taking place in the world around us but also the character of our internal reactions

to that change. Although human reactions differ, there is an underlying tendency among all of us to resist change, even to fear it. What
is it about impermanence that upsets us? There are several troubling
dimensions to the impermanence of everything. First, we can't always predict change. The inevitable uncertainty about the future that
approaches unnerves us. Our powers of knowing are finite and rarely
able to see into the future with clarity. We are regularly caught off guard
by what happens, even when we protect ourselves by remaining "on
guard" as diligently as we can.

Second, we may influence change but we cannot control it. It
frightens us to realize the extent to which we are simply subject to the
changes always secretly under way. We suffer impermanence in the
sense that it just happens to us in spite of our efforts to bend it to our
benefit. Like our powers of prediction, our powers of control are limited. We only occasionally succeed in dictating which changes come
into effect, and even when we do get what we want, it never turns out to
be what we had assumed.

Finally, impermanence implies coming to be and passing away,
birth and death. We see this happening to everything around us and,
at some point, realize that it will be our fate as well. All arising things
will also pass away. This is the primal fear built into our response to
impermanence—uncertainty, powerlessness, and the certainty that we
will die. So Vimalakirti makes this final point clear: "This body's . . . du-
ration is never certain—certain only is its end in death" (22).

How, then, does Vimalakirti teach us to live in view of this unde-
niable "mark" of impermanence on our existence? The first step is
simply to notice the ubiquity of change, to admit and accept the impermanence of everything we experience. Second, and more difficult, is
self-awareness, the introspective act of becoming mindful of our own
habits of response to change. Although none of us will be able to control the movement of change in our lives, it is at least possible to control
our response to it. This isn't easy, of course. It requires practice. It is one
thing to be aware of the changes around us and quite another to understand how our own internal patterns of reaction affect the impact of
impermanence on our lives.

Everyone who undertakes this kind of mindful self-examination
discovers internal patterns of response to the reality of change that

are unskillful and maladaptive. Dwelling on fear and insecurity without further inquiry into the roots of this fear and possible alternative responses just compounds the problem. Denial of the impact of change and self-deception about the risks entailed are just as disabling. To detach oneself from active life commitments by refusing to care or to disengage from life by imagining an alternative heavenly world of permanence just undermines the possibility of living skillfully through an honest, disciplined response to the problem. The range of unskillful responses to this most fundamental reality of human life is immense, and all of us indulge in them in some way and to some degree.

The *Vimalakīrti Sūtra* has its teachers offer a number of suggestions to anyone who has undertaken the self-examination required to observe their own unskillful habits of response to impermanence. The first of these is a certain kind of detachment. Vimalakirti teaches those listening to "regard all things as clouds in the sky, as the appearance and disappearance of a bubble of water, . . . as the tracks of a bird in the sky" (56). Meditate on the way all things within and without are passing through our minds, here now but sooner or later to change and disappear. In other words, don't turn away from change. Observe it, study it, and internalize what it means for your life. Teach yourself the arts of observation and letting go. The sutra's advice is to "purify your intentions" (26) in order to get "free of the habitual notion of possession" (25). Enter a "state of non-grasping" (29), "free of egoism and possessiveness" (45), so that what comes can also go and what has gone can freely be gone.

Vimalakirti takes this challenge himself, not by choosing something inconsequential to release but rather by choosing something that would surely inspire great attachment—his own wealth. He meditates on the reality of riches "without acquisitiveness and often reflects on the notion of impermanence" (65). He strives for "the joy of renunciation" (38) and the "perfection of generosity"—"to be joyful and without regret in giving" (57). But this renunciation, this detachment, isn't the cool, dispassionate letting go of the disengaged observer. Having taken the bodhisattva vow with passionate seriousness, Vimalakirti strives for full, active engagement, taking responsibility to use his resources skillfully to do what he can to improve the quality of life of those around him. He strives "to be responsible for all things, yet free of any possessive notion of anything" (27). And he realizes that to be generous in the act of effective teaching, a "true bodhisattva . . . must actively demonstrate impermanence to living beings who soothe themselves with the illusions of permanence" (69).

The "illusions of permanence"—what the sutra calls a "secure refuge"—are an inevitable temptation since anything, even the dharma, can become that object of grasping for security. So Vimalakirti teaches the monks—who each day pledge to "take refuge in the dharma"—that "the dharma is not a secure refuge." He says, "He who is interested in a secure refuge is not interested in the dharma" (51). Letting go extends to all things. The dharma is not a "fixed determination" that escorts you out of the realm of impermanent, interdependent complexity (65). It calls upon you to remain fully committed to life among the multitude of interdependent and changing beings. Therefore, the sutra has Mañjuśrī, the bodhisattva of wisdom, proclaim that "one who stays in the fixed determination of the uncreated is not capable of conceiving the spirit of enlightenment. However, one who lives among created things, in the mines of the passions, without grasping for closure, is indeed capable of conceiving the spirit of enlightenment" (65).

Mindfulness: From Observation and Self-awareness to Self-transformation

To be mindful is to be aware of what is going on within and around us in the present moment. With that broad goal in mind, mindfulness meditation teaches practitioners to be directly conscious of the contents of experience as they arise in the mind, develop, and disappear—at first without analysis, interpretation, or critical judgment. The point of the practice is to cultivate our powers of awareness, to wake us up to be more alert and attentive both to the world around us and to our own patterns of internal apprehension and response. The point, in other words, is to show us where we habitually dwell in mental space, which is equivalent to showing us who we are. Although common sense will insist that we already know that, the truth is that this self-certainty is an ever-present illusion. In fact, we often understand more about others around us than we do about ourselves. We can see other people, hear them, observe them from angles they can never see themselves. We can see the depth and contours of their moods while they are unconsciously in the grip of them. Self-awareness is far more indirect and difficult to procure.

We can think of mindfulness meditation as functioning on three basic levels—three layers of awareness. The first level or layer of the practice is awareness of the world around us. To be mindful at this level is to be observant, to notice sights, sounds, movements, textures—whatever appears to our senses. A mindful observer is alert, attentive to all dimensions and details of our surroundings. Picture Sherlock Holmes entering a crime scene, noticing hundreds of details that elude the rest of us. Mindful observers open their minds, allowing the world before them to make its impression.

A second level of mindfulness practice teaches us to be aware of our internal mental processes. It teaches us to notice the thoughts, feelings, and motivations that arise in our minds—whether in response to the world or not—and to examine these internal, often habitual, processes. These two primary levels of mindfulness meditation inevitably go together. The practice is simply to observe our own experience whether internal or external, since that dichotomy turns out to be so full of illusions.

There is a third layer of mindfulness meditation that has been crucial throughout the history of Buddhism. That is mindfulness of the dharma in everyday life. This third practice seeks to develop the capacity to be mindful of the teachings—to recall and to activate the teachings—in relation to the contents of experience that arise at the first two levels. This dimension of mindful meditation is about our values, our principles, our aspirations, our possibilities. It opens up from what is to what could be, to what should be. To be mindful in this sense is to have the guidance of *bodhicitta*, the thought of enlightenment. It is to be aware of our mind's encounter with the world around us in view of an image of who or what we aspire to be. It is to have that ultimate concern or foremost set of concerns close at hand as we move through daily experience so that the decisions we make really do show the impact of that aspiration.

This aspect of mindfulness serves to build and to maintain our integrity, to keep us on the path we have chosen and to resist the pull of circumstances that might undermine our values. Although the first level of mindfulness practice, and to some extent the second level, is to be practiced in a non-judgmental state of mind, that is far from the case at this third level, where the quality of our mental discernment and judgment is essential. But notice that this third layer of mindfulness isn't separate, cordoned off from the first two. All three layers of mindfulness are intertwined, empowering us to be mindful of our values in direct relation to what we are dealing with in the world and in our minds. It is to have our highest values impressed upon the situation we face in the present moment. It is to remember from moment to moment that we are on a path of our own choosing and that we are sustained by the strength of a conviction, the commitment of a vow.

One noteworthy meditation teaching encourages us to pay particular attention to eight distinct reactive patterns, called the "eight winds" because they have enormous influence in pushing us in directions that we may not have consciously chosen. The eight winds come in four pairs: gain and loss, fame and disrepute, praise and blame, pleasure and pain. These central concerns provide the motivational force behind most of our activities. We constantly seek personal gain and avoid loss, love fame and despise disrepute. We seek praise at almost any cost and do whatever we can to escape blame, while the winds of life blow us toward pleasure and away from pain with gale-like intensity.

The disciplined practice of mindfulness meditation provides us with something like an inventory of our own personal habits in seeking gain, fame, praise, and pleasure while avoiding their opposites. It opens an introspective mental space that lays these reactive patterns out before us for examination. The wonderful irony of this practice is that as soon as we are aware of our own reactive tendencies under these eight influences, we have already taken at least one step away from enslavement to them. The simple practice of attention is that one step back from immediately doing what instinct has up until now made us do. The third level of mindfulness practice works in the space opened up by mindful examination of our inner patterns of grasping and aversion. When we are aware of our mindless grasping for gain, fame, praise, and pleasure and our instinctual aversions to their opposites, and in the light shed by our highest aspirations—for wisdom, for compassion, for freedom—we find that the motivational power of the eight winds is undermined and diminished.

So, when the sutra describes Vimalakirti passionately engaged in difficult debate or in numerous situations in which any of the eight winds might have swept him away, we can imagine him at some much earlier stage disciplining himself in the basic skills of mindfulness. We can picture him having worked through Buddhist meditation practices similar to these, enabling him gradually to evolve out of ordinary reactive patterns and into the extraordinarily skillful bodhisattva that the sutra describes. Reading the sutra, we sense that Vimalakirti is deeply observant of the world around him, alert to the contours of his own response patterns, and not just mindful of but riveted on the higher values and aspirations that for many years he has been downloading from the treasury of Buddhist resources into his everyday life.

Meditations on Pain and Suffering

Buddhist writings and meditations address an enormous range of issues, but all of these point back in one way or another to a central concern for the suffering experienced by all living beings. Nothing affects our capacity for skillful living as much as the character of our response to suffering, in our own lives and in the lives of others. For this reason, Buddhist practices are focused directly on the way suffering is experienced and the way this pattern of response either harms or enhances the quality of our lives. They seek to generate a deeper understanding of the role of suffering in life and to put this understanding into effect in shaping our attitudes, actions, and reactions.

Different forms of meditation address the issue in different ways. Mindfulness practices teach us how to be aware of suffering in our lives as it occurs, how to stay present in the face of these frequent experiences rather than turning away. They teach us how to steady ourselves as the physical sensations of pain arise and how to overcome our fear of and revulsion at these sensations just enough to begin to explore and understand them. Closely related forms of meditation teach us how to respond to the suffering of others with compassion rather than indifference.

These meditation practices make it possible to learn a lot about our motivations in life, a lot about our own patterns of emotional reaction, and a lot more about how all of this inner character shapes the kind of life we will be able to live. Simple awareness teaches us how to differentiate between kinds of suffering. Some suffering is self-inflicted, and we know it. Eating all those sweets or drinking all those beers last night was the direct cause of sleeplessness and nightmares. Other suffering is fully impersonal and has nothing to do with our choices or actions, nothing to do with our personal karma. The universe is largely indifferent to us and when it rages, anyone in its path will suffer. When an earthquake, tornado, hurricane, or flood wreaks havoc on our lives, it does the same to everyone else in its path. Simple self-awareness also shows us how we experience the different qualities of pain. Some, like a stubbed toe, are easily identified and understood. Others, like feelings of inadequacy or lack of direction in life, are much more difficult to localize and encompass. Meditations function as introspective surveys of our experience. They provide clarity about the kinds of pain and dissatisfaction that shape our lives. Mindful of them, we familiarize ourselves with their underlying conditions and the texture of their play in our minds.

In its lengthy discussion of the suffering experienced in sickness, the sutra has Vimalakirti proclaim that "one is called 'bodhisattva' when one conquers the miseries of aging, sickness, and death" (46). You are truly a bodhisattva, in other words, when this conquest is complete. What conquest? In all of their conversations, neither Vimalakirti nor Mañjuśrī takes an interest in overcoming "aging, sickness, and death." What they seek to conquer is the "misery" that invariably goes along with these three most prominent hardships of life. Aging, sickness, and death, together with their opposites—youth, health, and vivacious living—constitute the substance of life. Together they provide the very meaning and texture of human existence. They cannot be eliminated from life without eliminating life.

Therefore, when Vimalakirti raises the question "What is the elimination of this sickness?" (45), his answer makes it very clear that he's not talking about measles, cancer, or COVID-19. He is talking about the "misery" that will inevitably accompany those literal forms of sickness. He explains that eliminating the sickness that he has in mind requires "the elimination of egoism and possessiveness" (45). Then he adds that this entails "freedom from dualism," and that for bodhisattvas all of this rests upon the cultivation of a profound state of "equanimity" (45). There is, in other words, a way to experience "aging, sickness, and death" without the misery that makes these dimensions of life seem so unbearable, and the sutra explains how to do that.

This distinction between pain-causing experiences and the additional misery that our unskillful responses to pain create goes back to the Buddhist parable of the arrows mentioned earlier. When an arrow strikes us, the Buddha explains, it hurts. When we fall off our bike, are the victim of theft, are openly criticized at work, are embarrassed at a party, or are excluded by our friends, we immediately experience pain. It hurts and our emotional reaction is immediate and instinctual. But when our reaction to that initial pain is rage, debilitating fear, deep self-loathing, despairing surrender, or any number of other likely responses, it is as though we go on the offensive against ourselves, continuing to shoot the arrows of self-inflicted suffering. Days after the initial incident, we may still be shooting the arrows of misery at ourselves, still fuming about what someone did to us. This could go on for months, even the rest of our lives.

This early Buddhist parable teaches us how to peel apart the pain of those inevitable first arrows from the suffering we cause ourselves with unmindful habits of response. One is unavoidable, but the other is, through practice, entirely avoidable. How? Vimalakirti just gave us the general answer. We can learn to avoid causing ourselves and others added and unnecessary suffering when we learn how to experience pain differently, mindfully, "free from dualism," by "eliminating egoism and possessiveness," through the cultivated depth of "equanimity" (45). Equanimity is the learned capacity to experience pain without added suffering. This isn't easy, of course, because by the time we're old enough to be reading something like what we're reading right now, those patterns of reactivity are deeply embedded in our character and neurological system. By the time we are as old as we are now, these reactions are unconscious and compulsive, unconscious in that we are not even aware of them and compulsive because we're not given a choice. We just respond the way we do and regard the added suffering that we have caused as part of the initial pain, without understanding the difference.

But in these teachings, both Vimalakirti and the Buddha show us how and why to separate the initial pain and the added suffering. They teach us that instead of total focus on the impossible task of controlling the world to prevent pain, we can learn to control ourselves so that further suffering is minimized or eliminated. Some Buddhists separate the two by using two different words, "pain" for the inevitable hurts in life and "suffering" for the eliminable self-harm that we tend to pile on top of the pain. But it is unlikely that this distinction will stick in the English language—both words will probably continue to be spoken in reference to both kinds of hurt. That's fine. What is important here is to understand the difference and to learn how to respond to one kind of hurt so that other kinds don't unnecessarily double and triple the misery.

The first step in this process of learning is mindful self-awareness, self-understanding by paying attention to our unconscious tactics of reaction. How do we respond to various kinds of injury in our lives? Each of us does so differently, but the primary point here is that we rarely know how we respond. We're so enveloped in our miseries that none of this has been taken up into the scope of conscious inquiry. Until we have examined our deeply ingrained habits of response through something like mindfulness meditation, we really can't say for sure what our reactions have been. To change this personal form of ignorance, we can begin to examine these patterns, over and over, until we see them with clarity: one type of response in these situations, perhaps another response in these other situations, and so on. To alter anything as deeply habitual as these patterns, we need to become experts on the character of our own mental states, and this requires that we engage in self-awareness training through meditation.

Although each of us has developed our own unconscious strategies of response to problems in life from earliest childhood on, there are clearly common patterns that we can recognize in ourselves and others. Exaggeration is one pattern that most of us share. We tend to overestimate the risks, pains, difficulties of our own bouts of suffering while expecting others to be able to face these same difficulties as a matter of course. Similarly, many of us resent the aches, pains, and hardships that are thrust upon us. We sense injustice in them and wonder, "Why me?" When difficulties mount up, we seem to expect an apology from life, and we adopt an attitude of resentful self-pity or sometimes blame. The sutra calls this "living in the grips of . . . resentments and their subconscious instincts" (47). "Living in the grip" of anything, we lack freedom to do anything about it.

Others escape into consoling daydreams and avoid direct confrontation with the suffering they face. They imagine themselves elsewhere, living some other life of invulnerability. Although their pain may have eased momentarily through this imaginary escape, the actual issues never come up for careful examination and therefore remain the same throughout life. Some of us react to mounting difficulties by disengagement. We just give up, refuse to take the risks of life, and withdraw into despair. A judgment is unconsciously made—life is a disappointment—when in fact the real disappointment has been our unskillful and slavish response to life. Until we have put this central dimension of life up to examination, all of us are trapped in one or another such reactive pattern that causes us to extend and to deepen life's suffering without any awareness of our own complicity in creating it. That can be changed through practice.

Vimalakirti proposes equanimity as a major dimension of the solution to difficulties with pain. But what would equanimity mean here? To accept the inevitability of painful difficulties of all kinds, to let go of our stern resistance, to relax our striving against possible suffering? In part, yes, but that can't be the full picture that Vimalakirti represents. Why not? Because the sutra pictures Vimalakirti working hard every day to make things better for his community. Rather than accepting poor schools, greedy economics, corrupt politics, violent communities, and widespread addictions, Vimalakirti is the quintessential force of resistance. His equanimity never means not caring. It never means apathetic disengagement. He cares, unconditionally. Equanimity doesn't mean that Vimalakirti reduces his effort to change the world, even a little. The bodhisattva vow to which he has committed his life is a vow to care deeply and completely and, in the end, to change everything. Far from undermining his energetic quest, equanimity enables it.

So, where does that leave us? It complicates our acceptance of suffering. It commits us to a life of labor to condition the future so that people don't suffer needlessly, unnecessarily, while simultaneously accepting the truth that suffering of some kind and in some degree will come our way in spite of our efforts. It commits us to cultivating the health of everyone, a sustainable and supportive environment, and a community of mutual understanding, knowing all the while that these efforts will fall short of their ultimate goals and that to some extent disease, environmental problems, conflict, and injustice will somehow reemerge in spite of our most valiant efforts.

It helps us avoid both detached, passionless surrender and frantic, counterproductive flailing when things get out of hand. It gives us a balance between resistance and acceptance, between effort and letting go, that provides the essential skills to live the life of pain and joy that has been bequeathed to us. It also gives us freedom, the freedom of non-compulsive identification with an honest and mature thought of enlightenment to guide our actions and decisions. Rather than being compelled by ingrained habits of reactivity that force us to respond to difficulty by piling more difficulty upon it, freedom gives us flexibility, adaptability, and resilience in view of whatever comes, be it pain or joy.

The bodhisattva vow to overcome not just our own suffering but the suffering of all living beings extends the concern over suffering indefinitely. The sutra puts it this way: "Thus, recognizing in his own suffering the infinite suffering of these living beings, the bodhisattva correctly contemplates these living beings and resolves to cure all sicknesses" (45). This resolution is enormous, obviously uncompletable. But it poses a challenge that we can begin to face by looking at ourselves with honesty and integrity. It makes us recognize and examine our deeply embedded tendency to cause suffering for others as a deluded way to compensate for our own suffering. It helps us see all the ways that we do in fact pass our suffering on to others through our unconscious reactions to fear and insecurity. It asks us to learn how we can respond to pain without inflicting further pain upon ourselves and others. It encourages us to go even further by recognizing the structural pain and suffering written into the fabric of our political and economic systems and to join the effort to eliminate these unnecessary and self-inflicted forces of destruction.

There is so much to learn and to understand about our response to and responsibility for suffering. But one thing that we can surely do and that Vimalakirti models for us is to become a living example of nobility in suffering. We can become examples to others of profundity and generosity in the encounter with pain, even the extreme pain of disease and death. We can resolve to take suffering in our lives as a discipline, an intentional exercise of openness that refuses to collapse under the pressures of great difficulty. We can form an intention to experiment with equanimity and openness in the face of troubles, to look directly into what we have habitually fled in the past. We can gather ourselves into a conviction to be a model of generosity and compassion when the chips are truly down.

These kinds of self-mastery are throughout Buddhism the mark of nobility of character, a mastery not over life but within it. And as Vimalakirti insists, this possible journey of strength begins in "the domain of introspective insight" (48) and comes to culmination through steady day-by-day practices of focused awareness through which we learn to "take pleasure in being consciously aware" (83). For the most part, there is nothing mystical or dramatic about the practice of meditation. The greatest fruits of meditation are earned slowly and steadily by bringing our minds back from unconscious excursions to focus on intentions that have been shaped in relation to a carefully honed thought of enlightenment. That is the wake-up call at the heart of Buddhist culture. In all these senses, meditation is Buddhism's gift to humanity.

5

Embodied Wisdom

Wisdom, *prajñā*, is the central theme of the *Vimalakīrti Sūtra*, just as it is for all of the Perfection of Wisdom sutras that initiate the Mahayana movement in Buddhism. To be wise, for Vimalakirti, is to be "enlightened about the true nature of reality" (36). Wisdom is the capacity to see past the superficial conventions that guide most people's lives in order to understand both oneself and the world more comprehensively, more insightfully, without self-centered illusions.

For Vimalakirti, this more comprehensive, more insightful understanding of the nature of reality isn't the whole story of wisdom, though, because wisdom isn't simply a matter of more accurate knowledge. Vimalakirti's enlightened wisdom goes down beneath the level of conceptual understanding to a transformed way of being in the world. His wisdom is the capacity to live in accord with reality, to enact that alignment with reality in everything he does. So although there are numerous occasions in the sutra's story when Vimalakirti's skillful teaching evokes a deep insight among those in his audience— a sudden opening of wisdom—that doesn't instantly turn them into bodhisattvas like Vimalakirti. They still have work to do. The transformation from an insightful vision down into the marrow of everyday life is a gradual, disciplined change that occurs through daily practice. Knowing something important—even knowing a lot—and wisdom are not the same. Wisdom is manifest as a way of living in harmony with reality that includes the intellect while going beyond it to encompass the other four components (*skandhas*) of human life. In that sense, authentic wisdom is fully embodied.

That wisdom necessarily encompasses the intellect, however, means that contemplative inquiry is one essential form of Buddhist practice. To fulfill this dimension of Buddhist wisdom, the *Vimalakīrti Sūtra* sets itself up as a series of engagements in insight meditation. From this we learn that Vimalakirti's quest for wisdom requires serious engagement

Living Skillfully. Dale S. Wright, Oxford University Press. © Oxford University Press 2021.
DOI: 10.1093/oso/9780197587355.003.0006

in "transcendental analysis," thoughtful inquiry in pursuit of truth about the reality in which we dwell. Although we all rely on wise guidance from teachers and insightful writing in this endeavor, that guidance cannot serve as a substitute for our own active participation, somehow exempting us from the practice of inquiry. The task of understanding is an essential dimension of Buddhist practice, even if every Buddhist must come to terms with and absorb the Buddhist teachings in their own way. Although it begins in insight meditation along paths of open inquiry about the character of reality, wisdom comes to fruition in all dimensions of human life, in a fundamental transformation of perception, feeling, motivation, and self-consciousness, along with thinking—the whole person, embodied wisdom.

Wisdom in the Realization of "Emptiness"

How does wisdom emerge in the *Vimalakīrti Sūtra*? It claims that to be wise is "to be enlightened with regard to emptiness" (*śūnyatā*) (36). Wisdom is sensing the "empty" character of all things and living in full view of that realization. Vimalakirti teaches that the bodhisattva's "home is deep thought on the meaning of emptiness" (67). Home is where you live, where you "reside" on a daily basis. Bodhisattvas therefore reside in the meditative practice of "deep thought on the meaning of emptiness" (67). When another bodhisattva asks Vimalakirti, "Where do you come from?," he replies, "I come from the seat of enlightenment." Then, probing further, the bodhisattva asks, "What is meant by 'the seat of enlightenment?'" (36).

In response to this question, Vimalakirti teaches the meaning of emptiness. He says, "The seat of enlightenment is the seat of all things, because it is perfectly enlightened about the nature of reality," which is "to be perfectly enlightened with regard to emptiness" (36). He says that "it is the seat of learning, because it makes practice of the essence," and adds that "it is the seat of liberation, because it does not intellectualize" (36), meaning that there is far more to wisdom than an intellectual conclusion. Wisdom, then, is initiated in the practice of meditative reflection on emptiness. But its realization is the capacity not just to envision and understand what emptiness means but also to live skillfully within it, thus to be comfortably at home with the empty quality of all things. Bodhisattvas dwell on emptiness in order to embody its meaning at a level far deeper than the conceptual, a level that also encompasses altered perceptions, emotions, motivations, and self-awareness.

What is the empty quality of all things, and what would it mean to dwell on that quality as a constant form of meditative practice? The empty quality of all things is that they lack their "own-being." Own-being (*svabhāva*) is a technical term in Sanskrit for things that are self-possessed and self-generated. The Chinese Buddhist translation means literally "self-nature." For anything to be self-possessed and self-generated is to have the nature of a true self, an immutable solidity that is unaffected by the world around it and therefore eternally unchanging. Such things are what they are on their own, without relation to anything else. They are not subject to conditions, influences, and change. Vimalakirti's Buddhist teaching, therefore, is that there is nothing that fits this description. Nothing has its own-being. On page after page, he teaches that all things are empty of their own-being; they are "without intrinsic nature" (36). All things are empty of an immutable, core selfhood. Nothing generates itself, nothing stands on its own, and nothing just is what it is forever.

Mahayana texts like the *Vimalakīrti Sūtra* synthesize three early Buddhist principles to define the meaning of emptiness: impermanence, dependent arising, and no-self. Insofar as all things are impermanent, arise dependent on other things, and for those reasons lack an immutable essential "self," they are empty of their own-being. The "being" of any particular thing is still just what it is, but it arises to become what it is dependent on specific causes and influences and it changes in accordance with the changing conditions of its interdependent setting. That everything is empty in this way leads Buddhists to refer to the whole of reality within which we live as emptiness (*śūnyatā*), in spite of the negative force of that word.

The sutra pictures Vimalakirti meditating on this theme over and over. No matter what comes up in conversation with others, he teaches them how to see what they are discussing through the wisdom of emptiness. Because the negative implications of this teaching are initially startling—everything is empty?—Vimalakirti occasionally clarifies to make sure that people don't think that he is teaching nihilism, the view that nothing really exists. His teaching of emptiness is meant to define *how* things exist—their existence is impermanent or changing, contingent because dependent upon other things to be what they are, and therefore without a fixed, immutable essence. Lacking their own permanent, unconditional being, all things continue to exist just as they are—to varying degrees in motion and transformation and always connected in various ways to other things that are also changing.

On one occasion, following a meditative formula in the Perfection of Wisdom sutras, Vimalakirti teaches that "material form is itself empty. Emptiness does not result from the destruction of material form, but the nature of form is emptiness" (74). The nature of all things is that they lack a fixed, independent nature, but that lack is what gives them the particular reality that they have. It doesn't destroy them, as Vimalakirti says here. It defines them as what they are. Another way that Vimalakirti makes this point is to say that "all things arise dependent on causes. Yet they are neither existent" (in the sense of permanent and independent) "nor nonexistent" (in the nihilistic sense of being nothing at all) (13). This is the way things exist: contingently, interdependently, and always open to change.

Why is this particular way of looking at things considered enlightening, the essence of wisdom? Why would continual meditation on this theme bring about an awakening of wisdom? This is the view that seemed to accord with the nature of reality, a reflection of the distinctly Buddhist view of the world. Early Mahayana Buddhists found no exceptions to the rule of emptiness. Everything does change in some sense and to some degree, and everything does come to be what it is in relation to other equally impermanent and interdependent things. This, they thought, is what the Buddha discovered and what led to his experience of awakening.

This view of reality, however, was not the primary point of the Buddhist path. The path was concerned with a fundamental transformation in the way people lived their lives, an awakening from ideas and habits that were rooted in greed, hatred, and delusion to a life in harmony with reality. They sought to live wisely, with insight and compassion, and to make this wisdom available to everyone. Moreover, something about impermanence and complex "dependent arising" implies that the goal of a permanently true and comprehensive conception of the whole of reality might be just another delusion, possibly just another way to live rigidly and dogmatically.

So although some version of this worldview has long been central to the practice of Buddhism, the Buddha and Vimalakirti both taught a degree of ironic detachment from it. They taught being careful about how you handle ideas, even very good ideas, even ideas whose truth you are in no position to dispute. Wisdom meant recognizing the finitude of all "knowing." It meant letting go to some extent, relaxing your grip, so that when change does come you still have the flexibility to realize it and to work with it. Meditating on emptiness seemed to require some degree of non-attachment, not just to everything else but also to emptiness itself. Even emptiness is empty of its own-being.

This may be the reason that Vimalakirti risked upsetting monks who came to discuss the dharma by telling them that "the dharma is not a secure refuge" (51). Clinging to Buddhism, using it as a shield against the onslaught of reality, a refuge from it, could become yet another sign of greed and delusion. That teaching can seem harsh. It pulls the rug out from under sincere practitioners trying to sustain their enthusiasm by telling them that at some point even their own Buddhist beliefs might become yet another source of delusion. Vimalakirti expands this teaching for the bodhisattvas gathered at his house that day by making the outrageous statement that "enlightenment cannot be realized, either physically or mentally" (35). Wait. Isn't that the whole point of Buddhist practice? Yes, and that's why the sutra's narrator reports that one bodhisattva, Maitreya—a future Buddha—was rendered speechless by Vimalakirti's statement on that occasion.

Enlightenment *is* the point of practice, but if you cling to any conception of enlightenment too rigidly that idea and that clinging will at some point stand in the way of its attainment. If you hold too tightly to the dharma for spiritual security, fixing it in your mind as though it possessed its own-being, you open yourself to delusion. Therefore, Vimalakirti says that he is teaching "the repudiation of all discriminative constructions concerning enlightenment" (35) precisely because, as he says, "enlightenment is the realization of reality" (35), and experiencing "reality" requires "the arrival at detachment, through freedom from all habitual attitudes" (35).

So even *bodhicitta*, the thought of enlightenment, includes a moment of letting go, an openness to whatever that thought cannot contain. The thought of enlightenment, like all concepts, all aspirations, and all things, is empty. It comes to be what it is at any point in time dependent on conditions, and it changes when those conditions have changed. Dogmatic attachment to ideas, although quite natural, perhaps even to some degree inevitable, is unwise. If reality is on the move, continually reconstituting in new ways, then unyielding attachment to ideas is just another way to lose track of reality, to misalign yourself in relation to it. That all things and all ideas are empty is not a denial of them, nor a claim that they lack value. It is instead a claim about how they exist, how their value or lack of it comes into being, and therefore how best to relate to them.

The Buddhist teaching of emptiness functions like a powerful solvent for the mind. It dissolves every mental attachment until nothing appears to stand on its own, nothing is frozen in time, nothing is static. Vimalakirti is shown in the sutra to be aware of the unnerving, difficult force of these teachings. He is aware that giving up the desire for permanent unconditional assurance might evoke "fear and trembling" in anyone who first faces this aspect of the dharma (36). It could be deeply unsettling, because if you engage these teachings seriously whatever was previously underwriting your sense of security could just melt into thin air. That unnerving experience of groundlessness is an important dimension of Vimalakirti's practice as a bodhisattva. He cultivates it intentionally along with other aspects of the dharma. The ability to look directly at the truth of emptiness—impermanence, no unchanging selves, nothing grounded in its own-being—without turning away in fear or evasion is the clearest sign of awakening, the clearest sign of embodied wisdom.

The sutra's word describing this aspect of Vimalakirti's wisdom is "tolerance" (*kṣānti*) (20). Through the arduous practice of concentration and mindfulness, by meditating on the emptiness of all things, thereby "overcoming the habit of clinging to an ultimate ground" (99), as the sutra says, he has learned to tolerate the truth about reality. Kumārajīva's Chinese translation calls it fearlessness. To encounter reality so directly that you can let go of deep, unconscious craving for security and certainty is finally to feel at home in the world since that is the true nature of all things. At that advanced point of meditative practice, Vimalakirti is pictured as fearless, able to live openly with the fact that both he and everything around him are always what they are dependent on other things and, because of that, always in motion, always contingent. The sutra envisions a bodhisattva able to stand up with confidence in a shifting world that is never fully graspable, a world with contingencies, contradictions, and dissonance—and to do that free from delusion. And then, beyond the capacity to tolerate this realization, Vimalakirti seems to let go of all that pent-up anxiety about security and certainty by experiencing the incomparable beauty of a fully interdependent world and the joy of liberating release.

Wisdom in the Realization of No-self

The *Vimalakīrti Sūtra*'s account of wisdom embraces and elaborates on the traditional Buddhist teaching of "no-self," the idea that there is no immortal soul or immutable self at the basis of each human life. Yet Vimalakirti, the ideal character that the sutra presents, is as unique and as vivid a "self" as anyone could imagine. Far from contradicting the Buddhist teaching of no-self (*anātman*), the character that Vimalakirti displays is intended to show what it could mean to live selflessly, without clinging, without grasping for an "unconditional ground" to underwrite one's life.

A reminder of the Buddha's basic teaching of no-self is provided right up front in the opening chapter of the sutra by a member of the youth group. Reciting to the Buddha in verse form, he says:

> All things arise dependently, from causes
> Yet they are neither existent nor non-existent.
> Therein is neither ego, nor experiencer, nor doer,
> Yet no action, good or evil, loses its effects.
> Such is your teaching. (13)

What is being denied in this teaching is a permanent center to human subjectivity, an "intrinsic identity" (36) that is self-established and independent of anything beyond itself. Later, playfully turning the irony of this idea around, Vimalakirti says that "the absence of self"—being "without intrinsic identity"—"is the intrinsic nature of mind" (31). Yet, as the preceding verse says, in spite of this denial of selfhood, "no action . . . loses its effects" (13). Even though "all living beings are without intrinsic identity" (36), life as we know it goes on just as it is without the unconditional assurance of an immortal soul. Indeed, without this universal dependence and impermanence, life could not go on.

What we think of as our "self" is, according to Buddhist teachings, best conceived as the coming together of five interrelated components—the five *skandhas*: a physical body attuned to the world through the senses, cognitive understanding through thinking, emotional reactions, will and motivation, and consciousness that is aware of all these components coming together as a particular person. Although the five components are conceived and translated differently throughout the history of Buddhism, the most important point is that what we think of as a unified self is in fact traceable back to these intermingling dimensions of our experience. No one element constitutes the real you, the deep self or immutable soul. Instead, the coherence of a person is thought to be the coordination—sometimes conflict—between these components as they shift and evolve over time. While perceptions direct our attention in one direction, feelings, thought, motivations, and self-awareness might coax it in some other direction. Our unified experience results from the intertwined movements of these five elements as they come to influence each other from moment to moment.

Rather than understanding ourselves as someone who *has* these perceptions, thoughts, feelings, someone standing back behind these components, Buddhists claim that we *are* those elements as they reconfigure experience at any particular moment in time. No permanent self resides beneath this continual realignment of components. Therefore, the teachings assert, there is "no self," meaning nothing permanent and independent to personally underwrite our shifting experience. Emptying the own-being of the self, however, doesn't eliminate the Socratic injunction to "know thyself." In fact, it makes that task of self-understanding all the more important, and this constitutes one of the central tasks of mindfulness meditation.

This form of meditation in the *Vimalakīrti Sūtra* focuses on "the realization of the emptiness of the five *skandhas*" (29). As is true of everything else, the five components are empty of their own-being. They lack permanence and independence. When seen as empty, each perception, thought, feeling, and motivation arises and disappears as it intermingles with internal and external factors. Long before Vimalakirti, Buddhists considered this meditative task of self-understanding to be crucial to their practice. As one of Vimalakirti's bodhisattva friends explains, "Understanding the emptiness of the five components is the entrance to non-dual wisdom" (75).

To get out from under the weighty delusions of self-absorption, Vimalakirti "advises cultivating the following consideration: Just as in the case of the conception of 'self,' so the conception of 'thing' is also a misunderstanding, and this misunderstanding is also a grave sickness; I should free myself from this sickness and should strive to abandon it" (45). The point of this meditative exercise is to help practitioners release the grip of clinging and attachment associated with inappropriate self-concern by means of correcting the delusive, commonsense understanding that presents things to us as objects for our personal possession. So Vimalakirti continues the meditative formula by adding: "What is the elimination of this sickness? It is the elimination of egoism and possessiveness" (45). "The dharma . . . is without the concept of 'mine,' because it is free of the habitual notion of possession" (25).

Selfless Existence

There are a few occasions, though, when the sutra seems to push too far with the meditative task of emptying. On these occasions it seems to overstate its case against the status of selfhood. Following a formula for meditation stated almost identically in all of the Perfection of Wisdom sutras, the *Vimalakīrti Sūtra* appears to advocate treating living beings as illusions. When Mañjuśrī, the bodhisattva of wisdom, asks, "How should a bodhisattva regard all living beings?," Vimalakirti turns to a standard list of similes. He recommends regarding all living beings "like the reflection of the moon in water, like a magical creation, water in a mirage, the sound of an echo, the core of a plantain tree, a sprout from rotten seed, the erection of a eunuch, and like the pregnancy of a barren woman" (56). The list goes on, a standard list for meditation at the emergence of Mahayana Buddhism since this same list in response to the same question appears in so many other early Mahayana texts. Each of these images has meditators introspect mindfully to examine how they attribute reality to what they experience. The sutra's goal is to demonstrate how these things are far less substantial, far less self-sustaining than we would have assumed them to be in ordinary experience.

Although the bodhisattva of wisdom would have certainly known the answer to this question—how should we regard all living beings?—he asks it anyway because he knows that this would have been a pressing issue in the minds of other listeners that day. But then Mañjuśrī raises the stakes of the dialogue by putting a much more difficult challenge to Vimalakirti. He asks: "If a bodhisattva considers all living beings in such a way, how does he generate the great compassion for them?" (56). Good question. If all living beings are illusions, if their existence is logically impossible, or if they are altogether unreal—like non-existent water in a mirage, a sprout that can't possibly grow from a rotten seed, or the pregnancy of a woman who is unable to conceive—then why would anyone care about them? How could you possibly generate compassion for them? What would inspire you to do everything in your power to help them live more skillfully after you've trained yourself to think of them as non-existent?

Vimalakirti's answer sidesteps the heart of this question by describing the extraordinary extent of love that bodhisattvas should have for all living beings, "love that is peaceful because free of grasping, love that is without conflict and violence" (57), and so on for a full page. These are profound images of love, each worthy of contemplation. But they don't address the force of Mañjuśrī's question—how can you possibly enact that love while simultaneously meditating on the thought that "all beings are like dreams, hallucinations, and unreal visions" (31)? You can't, it would seem, or at least, you shouldn't if the images you employ are so thoroughly dismissive of these people's reality. If you need water, it would be a fatal mistake to take a mirage seriously as a lifesaving source of hydration. Even though on the surface it may look like water, you should just ignore it, turning your attention elsewhere. So if living beings are like the water in a mirage, it would be an equally fatal mistake to love them with all your heart and go far out of your way to assist them. It might look like they're there and need help, but they aren't and don't because they are as illusory as the water in a mirage.

It's important to press this case against Vimalakirti's way of representing emptiness because as you read this sutra you can't help but flinch when the sutra says that living beings don't really exist, that they are illusions. That's why it is essential when reading the text to keep the definition of emptiness in mind. What does it mean to say or think that something is empty? Wisdom is seeing the emptiness of all things—that they are impermanent, that they come into existence and change as they do dependent on numerous conditions, and that therefore they have no own-being, that is, no static, independent ground. They lack a true self in the Buddhist sense of that term. So when the sutra claims that all living beings are illusions, what is illusory is the assumption that they are what they are on their own, permanently and independently. And when the sutra says that they don't exist, what doesn't exist is the kind of reality that our assumptions typically attribute to them—something separate, standing on its own, something with an "intrinsic identity."

The difficulty in these passages is that idea of "existence" in Buddhist languages implied substantial, unconditional reality. Things that change and don't stand on their own are regarded as non-existent even though there they are right in front of you. Non-existence is therefore true of everything, since from this Buddhist point of view, nothing is forever and nothing is fully independent. That's a major part of what no-self means in Buddhism, and coming to terms with that reality all the way down into everyday awareness is what meditation on emptiness is meant to accomplish. The irony in all this is that if living beings *were* unchanging and independent, if they *did* have their own-being, there would be no point in helping them because they wouldn't be capable of change. Only beings who are empty in this sense are open to the acquisition of wisdom; only flexible beings could awaken to a life in harmony with reality.

The liberating point of meditating on emptiness is not just that we treat people and things out in the world as though they possess their own-being, as though they are who or what they are on their own, independent of causes, conditions, and the changing flow of time. In addition to that, and even more problematic, is that we have deep-seated assumptions about ourselves that similarly assume own-being. What is it to live as though you possess your own-being? It is first of all to fully identify with your states of mind. It is to identify with whatever currently occupies your mind—thoughts, feelings, fears, resentments, and so on. It is a deep sense of ownership that treats these states of mind as though they really are you, clinging to them ferociously as though letting go of them would be detachment from your true self. It is to be mesmerized by ephemeral states of mind, grasping tightly to what would otherwise just be passing through, as though that's who you really are.

When our current mental state is attractive, alluring, we cling to it with anxious possessive energy. When we are repulsed by our current state we are repulsed by ourselves, unable to bear who we now conclude we really are. Vimalakirti calls it "living in the grip." "Living in the grip of dogmatic convictions, passions, attachments, resentments and their unconscious instincts" (47), we enter a form of slavery to an out-of-control mental parade. Grabbing ownership of this parade, we lose all capacity to work skillfully with it. It just is who we are, our own-being, and, with the high volume of drama, we experience ourselves to be stuck in this place permanently.

When faced with what right now seems overwhelmingly difficult, we fall into a mute depression. Disabled by the problems that feel like they are inevitable and here to stay, we refuse to engage in the tasks of self-overcoming because it just feels hopeless. Succumbing to suffering, we refuse to undertake a new beginning on the mistaken assumption that nothing will or can change. In this way we accept resentment and despair as inevitable outcomes rather than as unnecessary products of our own self-absorption and clinging. In this self-inspired tragedy, our "habitual notion of possession" (25) has come to possess us.

All of this is to say that the word "illusion" in these sutra passages creates something of an illusion, at least for us as contemporary readers, since it is precisely in treating all beings, including himself, as empty of own-being that Vimalakirti discovers how it is possible to love them and to treat their awakening from unnecessary suffering as ultimately important.

Wisdom as Freedom

Vimalakirti aspires to set us free of the mental habit of possession, which stands there in the center of our lives as an unconsciously adopted enslavement. And this isn't just Vimalakirti's aspiration. This insight goes all the way back to the Buddha, who had been credited with saying: "Nothing whatsoever is to be clung to as I or mine. Whoever realizes this, realizes the teachings." Working with meditations on emptiness and selflessness, the central Buddhist point is to be free of the deep-seated habits of " 'I' and 'mine' " (32). Treating ourselves as fixed in nature and self-possessed prevents both self-acceptance and self-transformation. Treating our minds and lives as open projects in which we have a crucial role to play, we avoid these self-centered illusions of both permanence and isolated independence. Renouncing our own-being, we are empowered to let go of the habit of posses-siveness. As Vimalakirti says, this practice "is without the concept of 'mine,' because it is free of the habitual notion of possession" (25).

The teaching of emptiness—the contingency and impermanence of everything—releases us from this pathetic state of affairs. It dissolves our compulsive tendency to identify with the roller-coaster ride of current mental states. It teaches us how not to lock in on whatever is happening as though it weren't fleeting and weren't subject to chang-ing conditions, as though we had no freedom of mind. Meditating on emptiness helps us grow into maturity. It helps us develop a relation-ship to internal states that is characterized by relaxed curiosity, fearless self-examination, and a determination to have a role in shaping our own lives.

The name that Buddhists often give to this fluid state of mind is equanimity. Equanimity is a subtle condition of balance, a skillful rela-tion between attachment and detachment, between disciplined effort and relaxed letting go. Pressing too hard on any issue can throw us out of balance, and in doing that make our efforts less effective. The ca-pacity to stand back from states of mind to examine them provides an even-minded imperturbability, the presence of mind to stay focused and attentive through the ups and downs of everyday life. Getting out from under the slavish compulsions of reactivity and into some degree of equanimity maintains the personal integrity that practice can develop. Equanimity breaks the immediate link between a strong stimulus and a compulsive, habitual response. It is a priceless form of freedom.

This freedom is not generated by indifference or passivity. Authentic equanimity avoids the dangers of acquiescence, resignation, and complacency, and it passes over the temptations of denial, dogmatism, rigidity, and inflexibility. Holding to a calm, mindful center, it sees passing images, thoughts, and feelings without identifying with them, instead putting them up for further examination or just letting them go. Exploring this dimension of wisdom, the mind functions without habitual preferences, able now to make choices that align with a mature thought of enlightenment. The Zen "mind of no preference" becomes a flexible center of balance and freedom.

The wisdom of no-self is, of course, closely aligned with the bodhisattva's vow. Vimalakirti's selfless teaching seeks to extend Buddhist wisdom to everyone, and his tireless efforts are repeated on page after page of the sutra without having him retreat into lengthy periods of self-care. Practice with and for others is his practice. His vow is to take the enlightenment of others as seriously as he takes his own, to care about their well-being and health to the same extent that he cares about his own, even if in each case his way of doing that might be entirely different. That reminder is important and comes up over and over throughout the sutra. It is not an account of all the ways that Vimalakirti perfected practices that would fine-tune his own enlightenment. Narcissistic concentration on one's own spiritual development is a danger that undermines the practice of self-overcoming. But that's the point of the vow—this isn't just about you and this isn't just about "your" awakening. If you awaken, what you awaken from is this self-absorbed delusion. The wisdom of no-self points to the extent that we are all in this together, all intertwined on a path that none of us owns or controls. Accepting that, and cultivating compassionate attention to the needs of everyone, frees us from the anxieties of overindulgence in personal spiritual grooming.

Finally, let's consider the extent of Vimalakirti's *prajñāpāramitā*, his "perfection of wisdom." What we're given in the sutra is an image of Vimalakirti as a bodhisattva who embodies every aspect of the excellence of character that the sutra's author could imagine. This is the sutra's composite image of the ideal—*bodhicitta*, the thought of enlightenment. What we're not shown are the difficulties that Vimalakirti would have had to overcome in attaining this degree of human excellence. The sutra doesn't reach back in time to show us the weaknesses that had to be overcome, the mistakes that were inevitably made, the doubts and depressions that Vimalakirti worked through to become a bodhisattva of such extraordinary standing. Focused on imagining a life of greatness for this fictional character, the sutra didn't show us how he got there. But it still leaves us wondering. If, as Vimalakirti taught, we're all "living in the abode of Mara," the world that includes turmoil, disruption, difficulty, and trial and error—all kept afloat by delusions of tragic misunderstanding—what story might also have been told about his personal path of self-overcoming? Plenty, no doubt, but that would have been a story for another sutra.

Keeping that qualification in mind, we should also remind ourselves here that no one ever earns complete exemption from life's difficulties, nor from suffering. No one achieves a final redemption from the human condition. That insight of honest acceptance is the brilliance of the Buddhist path. There is no immunity from the turbulence that our lives feature—there are only wiser, more skillful relations to these difficulties. Fantasies of immortality, other worlds beyond change and suffering, and lives without risk and decision are set aside in order to get down to the business of this life just as it is. We are always fully exposed to the world and never sealed off in protection from it. Dharma practice is a practice of ongoing renewal and enhancement, ongoing self-overcoming without end. Buddhist instincts are gratefully to affirm this state of affairs as our life and, based on that affirmation, to pursue paths through it with wisdom and compassion.

6

Skill-in-Means

The thought of enlightenment guiding Vimalakirti's life was centered on two primary Buddhist ideals, wisdom and compassion. Throughout the sutra, we are shown how these two ideals coalesce. Vimalakirti says, for example, that "meditation on emptiness is consummated in effectiveness in the development of all living beings" (40). This is to say that, in the final analysis, the wisdom of "emptiness" comes to fruition—"is consummated"—in carrying out real-life acts of compassion. But a key word in that quotation is "effectiveness." Wise insight into the ultimately "empty" nature of reality and a commitment to extend compassion to all living beings are both high-altitude ideals. They apply to everything, everywhere, no matter how distinct and variable these may be.

For anyone making a commitment to these ideals the question of how to enact them in real-life situations in the most effective ways must have been seemed crucial. Ideals and specific courses of action don't always come neatly fitted together. It must have been as clear to early Buddhists as it is to us that those people whose insight and vision are most comprehensive and those whose hearts are most open in compassion are not always the ones who are most skillful at putting that vision or that compassion into concrete, effective action. In fact, they realized, if the dharma is medicine for healing the wounds of human suffering, it is important to understand how best to administer the cure since, as we all know, medicine administered in the wrong ways, or at the wrong times, or to the wrong people can in fact have poisonous effects.

Bringing deep insight and compassion to bear on concrete relationships, responsibilities, and the pressures of everyday life seemed to require yet another kind of human excellence. Early Mahayana Buddhists called this form of excellence *upāya*, skill-in-means (sometimes translated "skillful means" or "skill in liberative

Living Skillfully. Dale S. Wright, Oxford University Press. © Oxford University Press 2021.
DOI: 10.1093/oso/9780197587355.003.0007

technique"). This skill is featured above all other qualities of the bo-dhisattva in the *Vimalakīrti Sūtra*. Although the sutra's articulation of the wisdom (*prajñā*) of emptiness (*śūnyatā*) is both very sophisticated and central to its teaching, it is not especially innovative since it aligns closely with how these crucial insights emerge in the Perfection of Wisdom sutras. Vimalakirti's innovation comes in the extension of the wisdom of emptiness into the skillful means of applying it in a broad range of settings. *Upāya* is the creative edge of the *Vimalakīrti Sūtra*.

So let us define it broadly to begin. The skill of *upāya* is the capacity to bring insight about the empty nature of reality to bear on everyday life situations under the influence of a wide range of circumstances. It is the ability to apply the highest Buddhist values of wisdom and com-passion to the always changing conditions of real life in the most effec-tive way. For Vimalakirti, integrating these lofty realizations with the practical wisdom of skillful means was crucial. Therefore, one of the very first things the sutra says about Vimalakirti is that he "integrated realization with skill-in-means" (20). This is the sutra's way of saying that Vimalakirti's realization of the truth of emptiness was as valid in practice as it was in principle, and that it is not enough to have high-level meditative insight and vision unless that realization is also actual-ized in the real world of unforeseen and difficult circumstances. We all experience this same tension in our own lives, the tension between our ideals or principles and the need to apply them effectively under chan-ging conditions. We all need skill-in-means just as much as we need a vision to inspire us and to give us perspective on life.

The Buddhist commitment to focus on the complexities of life in this world rather than on afterlife in a heavenly world beyond this one brings the issue of practical wisdom to the fore. And Vimalakirti's personal decision to forgo monastic retreat from the chaotic messi-ness of ordinary life provides even more justification for the central role given to skill-in-means. The sutra pictures Vimalakirti working in the schools, involved in political debate, and fully engaged wher-ever divergent interests and serious disagreements might lead to con-flict. Wherever calm presence and effective reconciliation are needed, Vimalakirti's *upāya* was in effect. Success in these settings requires the capacity to work with energy and flexibility with and for others without egotistical clinging to one's own views and interests.

To be effective in these settings bodhisattvas have to be willing to let the world's rough edges rough them up. So we see Vimalakirti out in the streets working with people of all possible backgrounds and temperaments, not in spite of all the difficulties he would encounter there but because of them. He purposefully immerses himself in the "abode of Mara," the world of trouble and suffering, without retreat. The Buddhist path offers no detailed formulas for how best to respond to these real-life difficulties. No one, not even Vimalakirti, gets to know ahead of time which strategy to employ or how things will turn out depending on which choice he makes. No one gets out of ambiguity and uncertainty in life and no one gets to avoid risks. Not even Vimalakirti. Skill in the means of life is learned through trial and error—with plenty of error—especially through experience absorbed mindfully rather than unconsciously. Willingness to fail and the ability to learn from failure are essential preconditions to the development of any skill.

There is an intriguing parallel to *upāya* in classical Greek philosophy. The Greek word *phronesis* refers to a type of wisdom relevant to worldly action and practical issues, in distinction from *sophia*, the wisdom to discern the truth about reality. Socrates claims that this practical wisdom is essential for anyone hoping to live successfully in a world of complications and change. Aristotle praises practical wisdom as a skill of flexibility that is required to understand how to act in particular situations, as well as a skill of persuasiveness among people of diverse backgrounds and capacities. All of these features of the Greek *phronesis* can be seen in the Buddhist regard for skill-in-means. The Buddhist *prajñā*, wisdom, is, like *sophia*, high-level awareness of the true nature of reality. And *upāya*, like *phronesis*, is the competence to align that overarching awareness with the complex and variable situations in which we live. These two ideas are clearly distinct since they function within the frameworks of quite different worldviews. But their similarities can be helpful to us in considering how these ideas might be applied in contemporary lives.

The *Vimalakīrti Sūtra* could hardly feature skill-in-means more prominently. As Vimalakirti says: "Wisdom not integrated with skill-in-means is bondage, but wisdom integrated with skill-in-means is liberation" (46).

Vimalakirti's Teaching: Community as an Art Form

We began this chapter with a broad definition of *upāya*. Skill-in-means is the capacity to bring insight about the empty nature of reality to bear on everyday life situations under the pressure of a wide range of circumstances. It is the ability to apply the highest Buddhist values of wisdom and compassion to the always changing conditions of real life in the most effective way. Most references to *upāya* in Mahayana sutras and in the *Vimalakīrti Sūtra* refer to how this skill takes shape in the act of teaching, that is, skill in the means or methods of communicating the dharma for the purpose of healing human suffering. Vimalakirti is praised for teaching the dharma with uncanny skill, shaping its transformative message specifically for the different orientations and capacities of his audience. It says that "having integrated his realization with skill-in-means . . . Vimalakirti understood the thoughts and actions of living beings, their strengths and weaknesses," and having understood them in their individuality, "he taught the dharma appropriately to each" (20).

This same context-dependent skill for nuanced communication had long been attributed to the Buddha himself. So, in a poem of praise in the opening chapter of the *Vimalakīrti Sūtra* the youthful poet says:

> Although the Buddha speaks with but one voice,
> Those present perceive that same voice differently,
> And each understands in his own language according to
>   his own needs.
> This is a special quality of the Buddha. (14)

The Buddha's skillful communication is a "special quality" indeed. People who understand the world in different ways and who have very different needs all hear the Buddha giving the same dharma talk, yet each comes away transformed by a message perfectly suited to their own unique situations. The first chapter goes on to say: "Living beings see the Buddha field according to their own degree of purity" (18). That's true in this sense: Everyone interprets and understands their own community and surrounding environment in accordance with their state of mind, in alignment with their particular character and the extent to which their minds are open, concentrated, attentive. How the world appears to them will depend on the degree to which they have managed to overcome their own greed, hatred, and delusion through explicit practices of self-overcoming. Also, there are even deeper orientations in life that make people different. People's minds are shaped by different genetic predispositions, different family histories and upbringings. They have very different temperaments, occupations, sensibilities, and lifestyles. They have different ideologies, different problems, different emotional dispositions.

The sutra praises Vimalakirti for his ability to take these differences into account in teaching the residents of Vaiśālī. What was he teaching them? Remember, first, that Vimalakirti wasn't just a teacher in our sense of that word. He was a healer, a physician, prescribing aspects of the dharma as medicine for a variety of maladies—personal, social, mental, spiritual. Therefore, he taught a range of different practices in order to address these very different issues. One reason the *Vimalakīrti Sūtra* is so interesting to us today is that we can hear not just the teachings themselves in a generalized version but specific teachings that Vimalakirti has applied to the specific problems or worldviews of different people. In order to do this Vimalakirti had to be a master diagnostician. All prescriptions have to match each particular diagnosis with precision. The problems that diminish human life are extensive and diverse: discontent, restlessness, lethargy, self-doubt, fear, hatred, anxiety, indifference, irritability, boredom, daydreaming, intoxication, sexual craving, egocentric desire for praise, resentment—and our list goes on and on. In order to be effective the teachings and practices offered would have to vary in accordance with variations in the particular problems faced.

Some of these unskillful responses to life have even deeper causes— strong visceral attachments that are emotional or ideological, or egocentric fixations that have worked their way deep into our bodies and mental fabric. That's lack of freedom. We lack freedom and don't even know it. We didn't decide to spend yesterday off in a fantasy world daydreaming, or bitterly resenting our family, or inwardly fuming at our presumptuous neighbors. We just did it based on habitual patterns that, lacking mindfulness, we don't even see; these are reactive patterns stored in our bodies and subconscious mind. But now that we have spent the day that way for whatever reasons, the aftermath is upon us. We don't feel very well—slightly anxious, experiencing some indigestion. We also feel smallish, hemmed in, unfree. Moreover, as a result of those actions, that same unconscious pattern of response is now more deeply inscribed in our neurology, ever ready to pop back out into our active lives the next time an appropriate trigger grabs hold of our unmindful mind. And we go about our lives without becoming aware of this pattern, much less doing anything about it.

We've digressed here slightly just to make sure that when we describe Vimalakirti as a spiritual healer, we don't assume that the "sicknesses" he sought to heal aren't among those that we face. They are. Everyone's different, but these patterns of human weakness and strength are relatively enduring in the slow evolution of human consciousness. So Vimalakirti goes about fulfilling his bodhisattva vow to work as hard for the well-being of other living beings as for his own and to do so with skills that are mindful of vast human differences.

There is irony—even humorous irony—in the way the sutra communicates Vimalakirti's teaching skill to us. Recall how the sutra's author has Vimalakirti pretend to be sick. Or he *is* sick. "I'm sick as long as anyone is sick," he says (41–42). The Buddha understands Vimalakirti's ploy—his skill-in-means—and wants to send disciples and bodhisattvas to go check on the invalid, knowing that when they arrive Vimalakirti will be ready to wake them up by exposing each of them to insights that address their particular weaknesses. But in response to the Buddha's request, none of these accomplished Buddhist practitioners is willing to go. When asked, one by one they decline the invitation, each telling the story of their own personal encounter with Vimalakirti. In every case they confess that Vimalakirti's dharma insight was beyond their comprehension and that they couldn't help but be impressed, baffled, and embarrassed by the brilliance of his teachings.

The sutra's author tells these riveting stories in order to accentuate the depth of Vimalakirti's wisdom in contrast to the Buddha's monastic disciples. Vimalakirti is a layperson whose dharma realization is so profound that his teachings befuddle even the most advanced disciples of the Buddha. But notice that, in making that case, the sutra inadvertently tells us that Vimalakirti's skill-in-teaching-techniques was deficient. If nobody is willing to visit Vimalakirti because they end up being humiliated and embarrassed in the encounter, that's bad *upāya*. In making a point about the depth of Vimalakirti's vision, the author also unwittingly demonstrates a serious weakness in his skill and adaptability as a teacher.

It is interesting that through the long history of Buddhism readers don't seem to have noticed this implication and move ahead in the story accepting the sutra's claim that Vimalakirti's insight is unmatched even though that same claim simultaneously reveals a serious weakness in *upāya*. But at this point, we should certainly notice. An effective teacher of the dharma would attract students, not scare them away. Students would want to be in the presence of a liberating teacher, and that would require that they not feel embarrassed about the wisdom deficit between themselves and the teacher, certainly not humiliated. Much of the most skillful teaching is done unnoticeably, in an atmosphere of ease and openness rather than pressure and humiliation. So we see here a limitation on the author's skill in teaching us "skillful means" through his creation of the otherwise brilliant character, Vimalakirti.

But by the fifth chapter the Buddha's problem has been solved. Mañjuśrī, the bodhisattva of wisdom, has agreed to go check up on Vimalakirti's health. As soon as it becomes clear to the others that it will be Mañjuśrī's reputation on the line and not theirs, everyone wants to tag along. It promises to be the dharma event of the year and thousands of monks, nuns, and laypeople, and even some spirits, gods, and goddesses, make their way to Vimalakirti's house to witness the spectacle. The ensuing dharma dialogue between the two bodhisattvas is brilliant, and the events that transpire at Vimalakirti's house that day are described in detail through five full chapters, the heart of the sutra. The skill of Vimalakirti's teaching is truly unmatched, although others, especially Mañjuśrī, also emerge as incredibly effective transmitters of the dharma.

Vimalakirti fulfills his bodhisattva vow by becoming a "benefactor of all living beings" (39). He "serves as a bridge and a ladder for all people" (64) to cross over into the mental state of nirvana and to elevate their capacity for mindful wisdom and compassion. He teaches spiritual practices of discernment and transformation. He teaches inner exploration, inquiry, and openness of mind. He inspires energetic, focused striving as well as "letting go," the release of awakening.

When Vimalakirti vows to share other people's suffering he also commits to sharing in their recovery and awakening. To do this he must strive to be "responsible for all things yet free of possessive notions" (27). He must "develop men and women while keeping their emptiness in mind" (26). He seeks to inspire an almost erotic striving toward ecstatic "joy in the pleasures of the dharma" (37). Perched on the "seat of enlightenment," he works "the means of unification" because it "brings all living beings together" into a community of sharing (36). Vimalakirti vows to embody the "four means of unification—generosity, kindness, helpfulness, and consistency between words and deeds"—in order to foster a community of awakening (16). He works with his community to create something truly healthy for all, something beautiful for everyone. Vimalakirti is a healer whose vow is to practice community as an art form.

In doing all this through his teaching, Vimalakirti realizes that "even the expression 'to teach the dharma' is presumptuous" (23). Presumptuous how? Most importantly, no one—no finite person—could live up to this billing. The dharma is always, by definition, beyond our current capacity. That's just what our highest ideals are—measures that stretch human imagination of what we could be out to our current limits. Those who pride themselves on their "dharma skill" can't help but be presumptuous. In view of that presumption, we see Vimalakirti always working back and forth between the effort to teach verbally and the instinct to teach by way of silent equanimity.

Intention: Practicing "High Resolve"

Vimalakirti is skillful at inspiring the development of intention—commitment to some ideal course of action with conviction, what the sutra calls "high resolve" (36). Intentions that are explicit and chosen through careful deliberation give orientation to lives that are otherwise more or less aimless. Intentions form a path of purpose. They stake out aspirations strong enough to order a person's priorities. They motivate and empower real choices. Without explicit intention, we slip aimlessly through life avoiding resistance and pain while grasping for pleasure. Desires follow unconscious causes, while intentions follow conscious reasons.

Intentions in this sense are the key to personal freedom. Only through self-aware, mindful intention do we really get to make a choice. Otherwise, predispositions, ingrained habits, and well-ensconced compulsions lead the way and we just follow along. Lacking mindful self-scrutiny, we don't even know what motivates us to act. We clearly do things, want things, resist things, but these actions aren't based on purposes we have chosen. Motivations of this sort aren't really intentions. They are reactive patterns that have come to be stored in our bodies and inscribed in our minds through long-standing habit. They are motives buried beneath the level of consciousness, inaccessible and unknown to us. Mental default settings of this kind are prior to intentional cultivation of character and, because of that, shaped by impulses of all kinds, including greed, hatred, and delusion, the three poisons that make us push and pull chaotically through life. In this sense we don't get to play an active role in our own lives until we have developed the skillful capacity to form intentions clear enough and strong enough to direct our actions. This is what "high resolve" means for Vimalakirti.

From a Buddhist point of view, the most important of these intentions is the "thought of enlightenment" (*bodhicitta*), the key to Buddhist practice that was introduced in the opening chapter of the *Vimalakīrti Sūtra*. The thought of enlightenment isn't just any plan or intention. It is the overarching intention, the highest value, one's ultimate concern in life. *Bodhicitta* is the ideal in view of which all choices should be made, the concern against which all other concerns can be evaluated. In Mahayana Buddhism, the model for *bodhicitta* provided by the tradition is the bodhisattva vow. Vimalakirti repeats this vow throughout the sutra, phrasing it in as many ways as the author can imagine. That vow is to seek comprehensive human enlightenment through mindful practices crafted to cultivate wisdom and compassion. It is to become a "benefactor of all living beings" and to become skillful enough in the pursuit of this vow to be "effective in the development of all living beings" (39).

The word "vow" adds a dimension of conviction to our word "intention." We intend many things but when we take a vow we go further in committing ourselves to a course of action. In Buddhism, *bodhicitta* is taken with vow-like seriousness. But in return the thought of enlightenment functions to do something to us. It inspires and energizes, it opens an imaginable path forward and evokes the power and the freedom to do something that we were previously unable to do—to discipline ourselves in the service of a concern that strikes us as having ultimate validity.

Vimalakirti calls it "the great path" (28) because it encompasses everyone and everything. It is so great that it is obvious to everyone that it cannot be accomplished, at least not now or in the near future. And certainly not by me. Its greatness—the "Maha" in Mahayana—is that it is ultimately a goal and aspiration in which everyone will need to participate. The bodhisattvas' vow is to devote themselves completely and wholeheartedly toward an end that they cannot fully imagine at the outset, and to do so not just out of their own willpower but inspired and empowered by a vision that stands out beyond them.

That's the overarching intention—the thought of enlightenment that Vimalakirti's teaching seeks to evoke. But having an overarching ideal or aspiration doesn't provide the down-to-earth directives that someone would need to get anything moving in that direction. A thought of enlightenment is a big-picture goal—in this case the largest possible goal—that now needs to be filled out in terms of intentions at many other levels. In response to Vimalakirti's effort to inspire "high resolve" (36), in our time we can imagine a high-resolution digital image, a visual image of greater and greater depth and detail. Down beneath an overarching vision, then, the goal would be further differentiated into various dimensions, each filled out with nuanced directives for what could be done in particular to advance the overall project.

Although bodhisattva vows may all aim in the same direction, the particular intentions of each bodhisattva would inevitably vary. We all work out of our own background, our own genealogy and family heritage, our own dispositions, characters, and problems. No one can just start from scratch wherever they choose. We have no choice but to begin right where we are, with all of the trajectories and all of the issues that have already shaped our lives. In each case, everything past must now be integrated in relation to a larger vision of what life is about. In Vimalakirti's case, that background is his career as a businessperson, an entrepreneur, a landlord, and more. So his thought of enlightenment is sometimes articulated in the language of enterprise. Of "true bodhisattvas," Vimalakirti says:

> Their wealth is the holy dharma,
> And their business is its teaching,
> Their great income is pure practice,
> And it is dedicated to the supreme enlightenment. (68)

This is the diction of Vimalakirti's everyday life, but now completely dedicated to the fulfillment of an avowed thought of enlightenment. His purposes in business have been transformed, given new direction and meaning. The point of his profit is not just the security and well-being of his family but the well-being of all living beings. Few other bodhisattvas would have expressed their commitment in these business-oriented terms. They would have their own background to integrate and to transform. This one is specific to Vimalakirti. He doesn't abandon the life he has built when he enters the Buddhist path because that's who he is. Instead, he transforms it by infusing every dimension of that life with the ideals of his vow.

This is one way to say that although the Buddhist path is there for adoption, it needs to be recreated, developed, and cultivated anew each time someone finds themselves inspired by a thought of enlightenment. Thus the "buddha-field" the sutra imagines is necessarily a field of differentiated intentions, at first our own varied intentions and then others'. Our action-generating intentions need to be harmonized in some sense with all the parallel or competing intentions held by others around us. Concerns of an ultimate nature are both fully personal and necessarily communal.

But you can't go through life with your mind constantly focused on the big picture. If you do, you are unlikely to ever get anything done. For Vimalakirti, that's unskillful. To accomplish your work you need specific plans, details of what you will do *today*, not just ultimately. Of course, if what you do today isn't a reflection of the big picture, you're just wasting your time—and your freedom.

Vimalakirti's skill was the capacity to work back and forth between the two, to envision the full scope of the thought of enlightenment and to carry out the next step in a concrete set of intentions inspired by ultimate ideals. He bears down to carry out some specific intention but occasionally pulls back from activities to reassess, to evaluate how current activities align with his vow. In this way Vimalakirti restores perspective by checking to see whether his overall thought of enlightenment is being obscured or fulfilled by the direction of individual acts.

In the poem cited earlier, Vimalakirti goes on to say of "true bodhisattvas" that their vow of compassion is their "vehicle." "Their driver is *bodhicitta*"—the thought of enlightenment—"and their path is the eightfold path" (67). The thought of enlightenment impels them forward, driving them by inspiring energy, effort, and courage. But the wide path it drives them along is the basic eightfold path of Buddhism, which names all the different dimensions of life that are open to meditative cultivation: one's view, intention, speech, action, livelihood, effort, mindfulness, and concentration. It's hard to think of any part of life that is not included here in some way. Everything is open to mindful transformation in view of a thought of enlightenment that provides guidance along the way. Self-overcoming and awakening would optimally occur in every aspect of life and always in ways that are individually contoured and personal.

On one occasion, Vimalakirti asks the Buddha's monastic disciples whether their specific practices of renunciation haven't obscured the big picture (32). He asks them to stand back to evaluate what they are renouncing. Are they renouncing the material world, ordinary society, sex, possessions? Or are they renouncing the way they have gone about relating to those realities? He suggests that to be "truly renunciant," rather than superficially so, is to be "without grasping, and free of the habits of 'I' and 'mine'" (32). Renunciation may at first entail literally giving up what you really do desire. But ultimately it is an internal act of freedom, and this, he explains, occurs through the cultivation of the thought of enlightenment at higher and higher levels of insight. Over time, these practices alter what you want so that "renunciation" ceases to be the right word to describe your acquired disinterest.

Vimalakirti adds yet another dimension of practice, that of "purifying your intentions" (26), an ongoing process of developing personal vision and agency with greater and greater nuance. It entails reimagining particular intentions to fill out and refine the big picture, the thought of enlightenment. Although the thought of enlightenment functions as a compass, a map for the journey, a stabilizer in the midst of everyday life, and a ground or foundation, it eventually reveals its own true status as a temporary or "empty" (rather than ultimate) ground. Impermanence is the true nature of everything, even our best intentions. We all secretly desire unconditional assurance that our own ideals and plans are ultimately justifiable. We would like to be fully confident that our efforts are perfectly on track and that our plans are beyond doubt. But Vimalakirti warns us about this "habit of clinging to an ultimate ground," a habit that he says must be continually overcome (99).

We can see the requirement to stand back and reconsider our vow in his phrase "high resolve" (36). To "re-solve" and to make a "resolution" is to go back and do it again. And again. The self-overcoming implied in the *pāramitās*—the six perfections of character—means that all thoughts are finite, even the thought of enlightenment. All aspirations need to be reshaped and redesigned, even the aspiration for universal enlightenment. Clinging firmly to our plans and intentions, we get stuck in place. Some degree or quality of detachment from our own past vision and plans provides the freedom needed to rebalance in the present on behalf of the future. This detachment in the domain of practice isn't a lack of conviction. It is a balanced way to let go of clinging and to loosen the internally possessive labels of "I" and "mine" that we affix to conceptions and intentions that are vulnerable to static habituation.

No one should pretend that this balance of committed engagement and critical disengagement (compassion and emptiness) is easy to maintain. Getting just the right alignment between energetically carrying out your best intentions and standing back from these commitments in thoughtful reassessment is difficult at best. But that is exactly the challenge. Once the insight of emptiness—that all things are finite, contingent, and impermanent—works its way from the easy things up to your highest and most cherished values, there is a reckoning that must occur. Vimalakirti shows us what a skillful balance between these two poles would entail, and how, once it is attained, rebalance would be an ongoing and regularly necessary act of self-overcoming.

The Master Craftsperson

Although Vimalakirti was an aristocrat and a businessperson rather than a warrior, the sutra says that "he was honored as the warrior among warriors because he cultivated endurance, determination, and fortitude" (21). Ordinary people, those who have no time for the luxuries of aristocratic self-indulgence, had great respect for Vimalakirti because he disciplined himself in the endurance and determination that ordinary people need to live without elite privileges. Therefore, the sutra goes on to say that "he was honored as the aristocrat among aristocrats because he suppressed pride, vanity, and arrogance" (21). Lacking the pride, vanity, and arrogance seemingly inevitable in aristocratic life, Vimalakirti lived skillfully among the common people of Vaiśālī. "He was compatible with ordinary people," the sutra says, "because he appreciated the excellence of ordinary merits" (21).

What were the "excellences" of ordinary people that Vimalakirti learned to appreciate? These excellences would have constituted a very different set of skills from those characteristic of the aristocracy. In addition to showing ethical skills like generosity and self-discipline that can be found in any socioeconomic class, ordinary people farmed, made wagons, baked bread, built houses, sewed garments, turned ceramics, and played musical instruments, domains of skill in which the aristocrats would have been clueless. Among the craftspeople who practiced these skills were those whose attainments stood out. Their skills and their products went well beyond ordinary levels of quality. They attained the highest standards of excellence in these cultural domains.

The sutra pictures Vimalakirti as someone who recognized excellence when he saw it in any sphere. Having overcome aristocratic arrogance, Vimalakirti saw in these achievements all the determination, mindfulness, and vision that distinguished certain aristocrats from others. He appreciated the concentration and self-discipline required to become a master baker, carpenter, or ceramicist and saw in these skills the fundamental ingredients of character that he expected to see in the greatest bodhisattvas. All of these people had cultivated the virtues necessary to master their craft.

Through the discipline of practice, they demonstrated command of a specific area of expertise at the highest level. Although the outcomes of their excellence—their products—evoked awe and admiration, there is nothing glamorous about the repetitive learning that led up to that achievement. No one is born a master craftsperson. They have no choice but to earn their exalted status through years of disciplined practice. These skills must be acquired, literally incorporated into their bodies and minds through tedious, unoriginal repetition. The work of apprenticeship in any craft is slow and arduous. It requires following rather than leading, and lacks the aura of originality and excitement that their ultimate attainment evokes.

Besides the discipline of practice, what is required to attain the level of excellence of a master craftsperson in any domain? In addition to the personal skills we have so far discussed, here are five that are featured in the *Vimalakīrti Sūtra*.

- *Humility or selflessness as an uninflated sense of self.* Vimalakirti's rapport with the common people of Vaiśālī is a reflection of his humility. Rather than boasting about his superior knowledge or aristocratic standing, Vimalakirti shows appreciation for the merits of others and treats everyone with profound respect. When advising a monk on how to enter a town with humility to beg for food, Vimalakirti says: "You should enter homes as if entering the family of the Buddha" (26). Addressing all people with the utmost respect, Vimalakirti recommends treating everyone as you would treat the Buddha—by honoring them with unforced humility. This humility is not so much lack of awareness of his accomplishments as it is a disciplined clarity about the immense scope of reality that puts everything in perspective, along with an honest awareness of his inevitable weaknesses. Overcoming his sense of self-importance, Vimalakirti models what it would be to live fully aware of one's infinitesimal position in the overall universe. Far from a shy habit of self-effacement, true humility is the result of disciplined self-overcoming that gives rise to visionary awe and gratitude. So Vimalakirti commits himself to living without "possessive notions" (27) and "without grasping" (32), "free of the habits of 'I' and 'mine' " (32). He opens himself to the world. This honest, uninflated sense of self provides the enabling basis for skillful living.

- *Facing risk with courage and wisdom.* An essential skill for effective living is the capacity to stand up courageously and thoughtfully to the risks of life. We all face contingency in life and, from moment to moment, the vulnerability that goes along with it. There is no escaping risk—of failure, of humiliation, even of injury and death—and we all know this intuitively even if we try to evade or deny it. Although these threats cannot be controlled or eliminated, what we can control is how we react to them. We can control our response by cultivating mental skills that enable facing risk by integrating all of our inner resources. When threats surface or when things go badly, responding badly is the greatest danger. Among the ways we do further damage to ourselves when difficulties arise are self-deception, resentment, a sense of outrage and entitlement, despair, and resignation. Living skillfully requires that we develop the personal power not to back down when facing the risks of life but to confront them directly and wisely. Living a healthy life of wisdom and compassion depends upon our skills in facing these inevitable risks. As the bodhisattva of wisdom reminds us: "Without going out onto the great ocean it is impossible to find precious, priceless pearls" (66).

- *Equanimity—balance and integrity.* If movement and interdependence are the true nature of reality, as the Buddha claimed, then imbalance, instability, and disintegration are essential elements of all life. Facing these destructive forces by accepting their reality while at the same time regenerating balance and integrity is one of the greatest challenges to skillful living. Balancing acceptance and resistance requires profound equanimity. Learning how not to be thrown completely off balance, how not to be unnerved to the point of incapacity, bodhisattvas develop equanimity in the face of turmoil and the freedom to choose wisely rather than to react compulsively. They keep their balance and maintain the integrity of their intentions in spite of unnerving levels of trouble. Equanimity provides the freedom to choose rather than to be compelled—to have the presence of mind to observe and to decide rather than to be forced. In the balanced posture of equanimity, bodhisattvas are mindful of pushing too far into excessive detachment. True equanimity is not indifferent. It is not distant, insensitive, complacent, aloof, passive, or acquiescent. In this mental balance, bodhisattvas are "responsible for all things yet free of possessive notions" (27). In equanimity they "abandon greed and hatred" (36). Equanimity stands for equality: "It is what benefits both self and others" (57). Cultivating true equanimity, bodhisattvas live with integrity, a state of non-conflict within themselves where the various aspects of life are held in balance.

- *Learning through mindfulness.* "Learning" and "knowing" are both verbs indicating action. But learning is an activity of openness, while knowing indicates an act or posture of closure. Learning is an ongoing process that may never come to an end, while knowing is a fixed state beyond which one need not go. Vimalakirti says that on the "seat of learning, practice is of the essence" (36) and that this ongoing "effort" maintains "initiative toward enlightenment" (39). Continuous practice builds experience, but the "experienced" person is not just someone who has had a lot of experience. It is rather someone who has been through experience mindfully with the intention of learning or developing. "Mindfulness" here is simply paying attention or, better, "being attentive." It is an intentional, focused state of mind that is present, conscious, and composed—in contrast to one that is unaware, dissipated, and scattered. Its openness contrasts with various forms of self-enclosure from anxiety to compulsive busyness to narcissism. Vimalakirti says that this meditative discipline develops "fitness of mind" and that the bodhisattva is "evenly balanced between mindfulness and awareness" (35–36). The "balance" named in that passage is subtle because it is "neither control of mind nor indulgence of mind" (47). It is neither a conscious grasping nor an abandonment of responsibility, but an openness of mind that fosters mindful self-overcoming so that the whole community of living beings might flourish.

- *Flexibility and improvisation.* The essential skill of flexibility—the ability to adjust, improvise, and realign with changing circumstances—isn't a random, intuitive gift. It is earned, a product of meditative practices of concentration and openness that put you into direct contact with the world around you. Residing in a sense of non-duality—the simplicity behind all the complexities of the world—lends the ease of relaxation, curiosity, and experimentation that avoids the exhausting struggle of anxiety-based deliberation. Vimalakirti likens it to "entering a state of non-grasping" (29), without the demands of "possessiveness," "free of the habits of 'I' and 'mine'" (31). In this zone of ease and freedom, he appears to make extemporaneous moves in the wide range of situations that arise and in dharma conversations at the outer edges of ordinary rationality. Improvising, he trusts instincts that have been thoroughly honed in practice, and he acts as though he really does feel at home in the world. On these occasions, Vimalakirti doesn't falter; he acts intuitively, without hesitation. It is as though he has been taken out of himself, like a child in play, where no signs of awkward ownership and grim determination remain. The anxious self-concern of tight fists and clenched teeth has been effectively dissolved. And although these skills of "improv" have been earned through disciplined practice, their sudden appearance seems wholly effortless.

These are some of the skills in Vimalakirti's toolbox of *upāya*—his skillful means. They are developed in the cultivation of particular intentions that coalesce in an overarching "thought of enlightenment." There is one caveat, though, that is reflected in these skills, and that is vital to keep in mind. This is that the skills of personal agency—our intentions, decisions, practices, and actions—are only part of the big picture. A minor part, in fact. In larger perspective, we recognize that "skillful means" and our title, *Living Skillfully*, might exaggerate the extent to which our role in life can be attributed to our own choices and actions. These phrases underplay the extent to which we are participants in something much, much larger than ourselves—from the rapidly evolving cultures of global humanity to the creation, evolution, and possible destruction of the universe in which we are housed. There are major dimensions of reality in which "skill" has nothing to do with it. Our small actions swim in gigantic historical and cosmological currents of impermanence that do far more than just encourage the direction of our lives.

With that in mind, here's the crucial point. As individuals, we are not responsible for the outcome of human history, the evolution of life, or the course of the larger cosmos. But we are responsible for our small share of the whole. That's our task, and that task can either be carried out skillfully or not. In that domain, we are fully accountable. And in that domain, the development of skill makes all the difference. It is vital to understand both perspectives and to put them into mental alignment. First, that we each have an individual life to lead, one that extends out into larger contexts. That's our primary task, our responsibility. And second, that ultimately it just isn't about what we do or don't do—reality encompasses us, overwhelms and embraces us. On the first of these we buckle down and get to work. On the second we let it all go, accepting whatever comes as a gift with wide-open gratitude and a mind elevated in awe and wonder.

7
The Goddess of Freedom

Among several alternative titles for the *Vimalakīrti Sūtra* we find "Sutra on the Unimaginable Release of Complete Freedom." Whatever else is under discussion in the sutra, it is always simultaneously exploring the meaning of human freedom. We find this theme prominently displayed in the seventh chapter, sometimes called "The Goddess" after its most memorable character. The chapter opens with Vimalakirti and Mañjuśrī engaged in high-level dialogue on how bodhisattvas "should live for the liberation of all sentient beings" (58). When that discussion ends, a goddess suddenly appears in human form and takes the role of lead teacher from here to the end of the chapter. Vimalakirti and Mañjuśrī step back out of the picture, while everyone in attendance eagerly awaits whatever new dharma direction the goddess will initiate. They're in for a treat.

Freedom Through Mindful Intention

As we saw earlier, the narrator reports that the goddess was "delighted and overjoyed" with the spirit of liberation emanating from the bodhisattvas' dialogue. In joyful celebration, she showers Vimalakirti's house with fragrant, colorful flowers, creating a communal sense of joy and wonder. Floating through the air, the flower petals slide gracefully off the garments of the bodhisattvas but somehow stick to the monastic disciples. Attentive readers sense that the sutra will once again try to articulate what distinguishes a Mahayana approach from what these practitioners considered to be outmoded ways of conceiving and practicing the dharma.

The disciples, monks engaged in this earlier style of Buddhist practice, are set up to represent the views and postures that will be criticized. Now covered in flower petals, they frantically brush their garments to

Living Skillfully. Dale S. Wright, Oxford University Press. © Oxford University Press 2021.
DOI: 10.1093/oso/9780197587355.003.0008

free themselves from what they consider inappropriate adornment. But the flowers are truly stuck. Or, as the goddess will explain, the disciples are. She turns to Śāriputra, one of the Buddha's most prominent disciples and one of the monks who had earlier refused the Buddha's request to visit Vimalakirti out of fear of embarrassment. She asks why he is so upset by the flowers now attached to his robe, brushing them off in so troubled a state of mind. Śāriputra explains: "The adornment of fragrance and color are not proper for monks and nuns who follow the strict code of rules for monastics" (58). All adornment, all attempts to beautify oneself, were forbidden by their code of conduct.

But the goddess disagrees. "These flowers are proper indeed," she says (59). The only "impropriety" the goddess sees in this situation is the mental act of clinging to rules indiscriminately. "One who is without such rigid thoughts is always proper," she says (59). As the goddess understands it, the flowers aren't really the problem. The problem, she explains, is inflexible attachment to rules, attachment that dogmatically forgoes clear-minded assessment of the situation. The goddess points to the others: "See how these flowers do not stick to the bodies of these bodhisattvas? This is because they have eliminated clinging thoughts and discriminations" (59). She goes on: "Those who are intimidated by fear of the world are in the power of forms and sensations which do not disturb those who are free of such fear" (59). To be intimidated by the world around you and to fear it is always to be on the defensive, never to relax that tense posture of anxiety and insecurity. And to be "in the power of" anything is to be compelled, to act without freedom as though living in a condition of slavery. It is to be caught in the powerful undertow of mental compulsion.

Here the goddess calls attention to two crucial dimensions of the Buddhist dharma: the practice of mindfulness and teachings on the cultivation of intention. The first of these is simply mindful observation. In this practice inner mental tendencies and outer behaviors are observed and examined. Mindfulness enables awareness of what we hadn't really seen before—layer upon layer of compulsion now ingrained by the repetition of habitual patterns. Prior to meditative inquiry, all of this is unknown to us. We just do what we do without reflection or self-awareness. Buried beneath conscious awareness are feelings, motivations, and simple habits of mind that continue to determine what we will do and who we will be. Mindful self-observation is the first step toward becoming aware of our own mental behavior, and that kind of self-awareness is the foundation upon which true freedom can be cultivated.

What the goddess offers to Śāriputra, and to us, is a way out of compulsive responses to the world's stimuli. You're clinging to the rules, she explains to Śāriputra, and that clinging prevents those rules from functioning in a liberating way by helping you look carefully both at the situations in which you find yourself and at the kinds of motivation that have habitually determined how you will act in those situations. The rules on adornment symbolize the kind of self-understanding that Buddhist practice is meant to awaken. They are reminders not to get lost in the pursuit of self-image, not to care so much about how you look in the eyes of others. But celebratory flowers falling out of the sky—what do they endanger? What is there to fear? Why conclude that the presence of flowers on your garments would diminish your moral purity? Lacking mindful examination of the situation, how can simple obedience to the letter of the law serve to activate the true aim of the law—the health and awakening of all living beings?

The "true aim" of the Buddhist rules for behavior is the second point that the goddess is calling to Śāriputra's attention. This is the overarching intention that should be there in the background guiding all actions—the thought of enlightenment, *bodhicitta*. In everyday life, this overarching ideal is carried out through numerous, more specific intentions—convictions about how we want to engage in transformative practice, how we intend to treat our families, our friends, strangers, how we intend to work, to exercise, to socialize, to eat. As we saw earlier, the eightfold path is an early Buddhist way of providing an overall framework for all dimensions of life that are open to transformative cultivation. It lays out all aspects of life that can be brought into alignment with the ultimate goal of a wise, compassionate, and healthy humanity. That's the inner aim of the rules.

What we consciously intend to do, conceived in conjunction with an image of who we intend to be, is a powerful source of motivation. But as mindfulness practice shows us, these conscious intentions are not the only motivators of action. We are also impelled into action by an array of inner forces that are largely unknown to us. Buried deep beneath our thoughtful intentions are habits, compulsions, feelings, and tendencies from past actions that move us to act in characteristic ways. These accumulated inner forces may lead us to act in ways that undermine our intentions, compelling us to act out of small-minded concerns like praise and recognition by others or out of resentment, greed, fear, or any number of other motives that we are embarrassed to admit. These are all internal motivating forces. Intention provides an alternative source of motivation. It differs from unconscious sources by being carefully considered and selected for a reason—that they align with an overarching goal in life, a thought of enlightenment. Intentions that are consciously cultivated over time accumulate sufficient force to counteract and sometimes to replace unconscious, self-destructive instincts.

As we now understand it, human evolution has granted us this power—the capacity to restrain impulses in view of a larger set of intentions about how we would prefer to act. But this highly evolved freedom is not a simple inheritance—it is activated only when cultivated, and the more we learn to work skillfully with consciously chosen intentions the more this freedom is enhanced. The path of freedom is an implicit challenge to each one of us: Can we learn to act out of motivations grounded in chosen aspirations—wisdom and compassion— instead of simply repeating small-minded patterns now ingrained in us? Can we form and maintain intentions that cultivate composure, thoughtfulness, flexibility, and resilience so that these traits become prominent dimensions of our comportment in everyday life? If we can, we will have established ourselves on the path of freedom, the highly evolved art of self-rule.

The Goddess Has "Attained Nothing"

At this point in the story Śāriputra seems to sense that the goddess might be right about the flowers and the Buddhist rules on adornment. He appears to realize that he may have been missing the point of his own practices of morality. He seems overwhelmed, perhaps embarrassed, and falls silent. After all, he's being teased and clearly outsmarted by one of Vimalakirti's guests, again forced to question his well-established Buddhist views, and this time by a goddess who makes her appearance as a woman. But the goddess just keeps pelting him with questions—like a Zen master wielding a stick—in hopes that her words can help him break through the narrow enclosure that he maintains out of insecurity. She says: "Elder, you are the 'foremost of the wise' [his reputation and nickname]. Why do you not speak, now when it is your turn?"

At that point Śāriputra falters and can only respond in a tired Buddhist cliché: "Since liberation is inexpressible, goddess, I do not know what to say" (59). Because silence is sometimes a sign of wisdom, when the going gets tough you can always just shut up in hopes that this move will be interpreted as profundity. But the goddess won't let Śāriputra slip by with this elementary platitude. She teaches him that liberation is neither within words nor outside of them, "nor can it be apprehended apart from them" (59). She chides his naivete in thinking that he can "point to liberation by abandoning speech" (59). Freedom isn't simply a matter of getting out of language. It is instead a way to reside skillfully within it without clinging in dogmatic closure.

But when the goddess concludes by telling Śāriputra that "liberation is the equality of all things," he stands firm, saying in effect, wait a minute, "is not liberation the freedom from three poisons—greed, hatred, and delusion?" (59). He's got a point. Surely that's the essence of freedom in the Buddhist dharma. If you're enslaved by greed, hatred, and delusion, you're far from liberated. But the goddess resists his point anyway, saying: " 'Liberation is freedom from greed, hatred, and delusion'—that is the teaching of the excessively proud. But those free of pride are taught that the very nature of greed, hatred, and delusion is itself liberation" (60). But how could that be? Liberation and greed/hatred/delusion have the same nature? Do those three traits properly characterize the awakened Buddhist? Hardly. So where is the goddess going with this point?

We can't tell, exactly, since she doesn't go on to explain. But let's explore possibilities based on other references in the sutra. The goddess says that those who claim to be free of greed, hatred, and delusion are excessively proud. That ideal of complete mastery over the human mind, mastery over all of the afflictive emotions, is in effect total mastery over life. But human beings, including awakened bodhisattvas, are finite, limited, dependent, and impermanent. Their self-mastery is always mastery within life, not over life. No one, not even Vimalakirti, the goddess, or the Buddha, escapes all obstructions in life. No living person eludes all traces of anguish, anxiety, aversion, anger, or distractedness. Just by virtue of being human, nobody enjoys a completely delusion-free life.

To take that "excessively proud" ideal as your goal in life is always to fail because it requires that you engage in escapist longing for another, superhuman kind of life, a life fundamentally different from the one you have been given to live. As living beings, we don't transcend our bodies or our minds. Instead the challenge is to live within them with insight, openness, and love. The challenge is always to live *with* contingencies, contradictions, tensions, struggles—all basic features of reality as we know it. The bodhisattva's goal is to live within these realities as free of ego and delusion as possible under current circumstances without regretting or condemning the kind of lives we live. It is to live this life in all of its complexity, without belittling what it means to be human. Not to face these difficult human experiences in some way is not to be human, and no one should aspire to that. Later the sutra restates the point: "Only those guilty of the five deadly sins can conceive the spirit of enlightenment and attain Buddhahood, which is the full accomplishment of the qualities of the Buddha!" (66).

If being human means that the dark side of human experience—everything from anxiety to greed, from aversion to distractedness—will always be finding a way into our minds and experience, what is it that distinguishes the mindful and wise practitioner from everyone else? Minimally this: that the bodhisattva will have learned to treat all states of thought and emotion as passing through the mind and that the compulsion to identify with whatever has captured current attention will no longer hold sway. Negative emotions and other troubling states of mind no longer need to be denied or defeated. Practitioners will have acquired the mindful skill of observing, assessing, and releasing these internal conditions without taking them to be who we really are, without being dominated by them.

Thus, there is no further need to either eliminate or succumb to the negative, no need to hate it, nor to feel guilty about experiencing it, nor, most importantly, to be devastated by it. At all points along the path these thoughts and emotions will still come and go, but increasingly without the felt need to be compelled or taken over by them. Since being open to the contingencies of human experience means that we only rarely choose what enters our minds or even how we feel about these inner images, the mindful condition of open awareness differs primarily in the loss of clinging. The acquired freedom of the mindful practitioner is the learned capacity not to grasp hold of nor to identify with what happens to be passing through. The Buddha's best advice was: "Nothing whatsoever should be clung to as I or mine—whoever realizes this realizes the dharma."

So when the goddess makes the counterintuitive assertion that the three poisons are not the opposite of liberation, she may have been reminding Śāriputra that the quest to terminate all experience of the negative in human life is just another form of delusion, a misguided quest to be something other than human. Such a quest is neither necessary nor desirable. In awakening we wake up from the nightmare of fearful clinging and mindless compulsions to possess and own. Yet life surges on, just as it is. And when the poisonous traces of greed, hatred, and delusion reappear, they may very well be the moments of trouble in life that finally open our minds and wake us up.

At this point in their conversation, Śāriputra is duly impressed, even if embarrassed. He says: "Excellent! Excellent, goddess. What have you attained, what have you realized, that you have such eloquence in the dharma?" (60). The goddess replies: "I have attained nothing. I have no realization. Whoever thinks, 'I have attained! I have realized!' is overly proud in the discipline of the well-taught dharma" (60). "No attainments, no realizations" comes down to "no clinging, no possessions." "Letting go" is mindful observation without grasping, without owning. In the act of letting go, we are released from the internal undertow of compulsion and rise to the surface for a deep breath of fresh air.

In Search of Her "Female State"

The dialogue between Śāriputra and the goddess continues for another page in the sutra before a characteristic prejudice slips out of the embarrassed monk's mouth. He says: "Goddess, what prevents you from transforming yourself out of your female state?" (61). There's a backstory to this desperate question. Although it would appear that the Buddha had little difficulty accepting gender equality with respect to the attainment of awakening, the patriarchal traditions of India (and everywhere else for that matter) would dilute that position over time. One way to avoid the brunt of the question about full enlightenment for women was to maintain that in their last rebirth before full awakening, highly accomplished Buddhist practitioners would return as monks rather than as nuns, men rather than women. This is essentially to say, "No, women do not attain the highest state of awakening because they would have been reborn as men at the final, crucial moment." Although this wasn't the official Buddhist position on the matter—there was no such position—it did circulate in some times and places as a cultural prejudice that partially undermined the gender openness that the Buddha appears to have held against the traditional wall of patriarchy.

So if we apply that idea to Śāriputra's question in the sutra, what he is really saying is, "Okay, goddess, if you're so enlightened why are you still a woman?" This question, of course, doesn't go over well. Energized again, the goddess pounces on unenlightened assumptions supporting that question. She says: "Although I have sought my 'female state' for these twelve years, I have not yet found it" (61). Is there a fixed essence that would permanently and decisively define the "female state"? She can't find one. The basic teachings of Buddhism claim that nothing is fixed, everything is impermanent. And because everything comes to be what it is dependent on causes and conditions that are changing and variable, nothing has a fixed essence, and everything is open to being something other than what it was before or is now. She wonders: Hadn't Śāriputra been training in this same dharma? If so, how could he conclude that static gender identity is an exception to impermanence and "dependent arising"? Does he really believe that awakening is an exclusive possession of men?

The goddess deftly poses a question back to Śāriputra: "If a magician were to incarnate a woman by magic, would you ask her, 'What prevents you from transforming yourself out of your female state?'" Śāriputra can only reply: "No! Such a woman would not really exist, so what would there be to transform?" (61). What both Śāriputra and the goddess mean by "exist" here is something that is permanent, something that exists on its own, in and of itself, rather than something subject to change under the influence of surrounding forces or conditions. The magically created woman would certainly not "exist" in that sense. So, the goddess pushes further to explain: in that sense of "exist," "all things do not really exist" (61). Nothing—not men, not women, and not gender—has a permanent, fully independent essence, a fixed nature that cannot ever change, be influenced, evolve, or be understood from other points of view. That, once again, is what it means for all things to be empty of their own-being. Nothing exists in that sense. Nothing stands on its own, always the same.

To drive the point home, the goddess conjures a magical display. The sutra says: "Thereupon the goddess employed her magical power to cause the elder Śāriputra to appear in her form and to cause herself to appear in his form" (61). Śāriputra now appears as a woman and the goddess as a man. With what we must imagine to be a wide, ironic smile, the goddess turns Śāriputra's question back on him: "What prevents you from transforming yourself out of your female state?" (62). He's completely flabbergasted, of course, and once again tongue-tied. She clarifies: "All women appear in the form of women in just the same way as the elder appears in the form of a woman" (62). That is, they appear in their current form dependent on past causes and conditions having shaped them that way, but when those conditions change, so will they.

Going a step further, she says: "While they are not women in ultimate reality [meaning not permanently, nor independently, apart from all shaping forces], they appear in the form of women" (62). All appearances are what they are in time, at some point in time to be altered by the shaping influences of causes and conditions. Bringing her lesson to a close, the goddess quotes the Buddha as saying: "In all things, there is neither male nor female" (62). Of course, there *is* male and female, but every single man or woman is what he or she is dependent on conditions. Moreover, what it means to be male or female is always changing in relation to cultural and evolutionary conditions that are on the move over time. Neither "male" nor "female" has a fixed essence, nor do all of the gender possibilities between and beyond those two.

The goddess's transgender fluidity helps Śāriputra to empty his mind of rigid ideas about gender identity so that the healthy conditions of gender openness can play a greater role in articulating the dharma.

Opening the Dharma

Let's step back from the sutra's storyline to notice what's happening. The goddess has altered the mood of the gathering at Vimalakirti's house. She has begun to open up dharma possibilities that not even the heroes of Buddhist wisdom like Mañjuśrī and Vimalakirti had been able to see. She has applied the Buddhist teachings of "emptiness" to an issue that nobody had previously thought relevant—the issue of gender distinction. And in the process of doing that with insightful skill-in-means, she has brought an element of Buddhist awakening into view that no one had noticed before.

Accordingly, the goddess's demeanor contrasts sharply with Śāriputra's. His firm stance of duty and moral fixity feels somewhat grim and stolid—a rigid posture that encloses the practitioner—in comparison to her lighthearted, open, and playful dharma mood. The goddess showers everyone in flowers. She sings joyful praise for the bodhisattvas' display of wisdom and compassion. The goddess's relaxed and beaming smile contrasts sharply with Śāriputra's tight brow and clenched fists. While he is taking himself far too seriously, she seems to move effortlessly and selflessly. The goddess rejoices in the bodhisattvas' conversation, and suddenly joy—enjoyment—comes into view as an ineliminable dimension of the kinds of lives that Buddhists should strive to lead. We may not have noticed that it was missing before, but it was.

The goddess playfully mocks Śāriputra's inflexible moral seriousness, his rigid application of the Buddhist rules, his incapacity to relax, his lack of humor. She seems to suggest that not only are women unnecessarily confined to a static and troublesome gender identity, but so also are men. She implies that Śāriputra's rigid and humorless posture of moral seriousness is an oppressive dimension of men's gender identity, and that this identity is, like her own, empty of intrinsic essence, and therefore open to transformation. If Śāriputra can take the opening she has offered and join in this lighthearted resistance to suffocating rigidity, he too can taste an exhilarating moment of freedom from himself by simply laughing. If under her influence he can just let go for a moment, feeling free to laugh at his own lapse into mental rigidity, then he too can experience the pleasure, the enjoyment, and the freedom of that release of grip.

Could she ever get him to laugh? The author makes no moves in that direction, but the episode reminds us that laughter does bring disillusionment—the overthrow of illusions—into our own lives. We sense that the bondage of self-deception is at least momentarily lifted in a deep, hearty fit of hilarity. In the elation of joyful lucidity, we see clearly what was previously hidden from view, and for once we get to laugh uproariously at our own delusions. Humor just puts everything into perspective. In this, the *Vimalakīrti Sūtra* prefigures the "dependent arising" of Zen masters some centuries later in China, where ease and dexterity of movement, extemporaneous discourse, and open, unselfconscious hilarity began to redefine what it means to awaken.

In a moment of relief from the clenched fists of serious dharma discipline, the goddess gives everyone at Vimalakirti's house that day some room to play. Aligning her teachings to the mood of the occasion, she suggests release, just letting be, a kind of freedom from our own will to control. She's right. There are times when our plans just overwhelm us, as though they are moving in to take control over our minds. Once adulthood is firmly in place and we become skilled at self-discipline and planning, the desire for control that motivates our plans and discipline starts to become a compulsion, an out-of-control desire. Tightly scheduled days pass by "uneventfully" just because we're not open to anything happening that might disrupt our plans. In this sense our plan to control the day allows nothing out of the ordinary to intrude, nothing that might disrupt the way we expect reality to be. Control becomes a synonym for closure, a lockdown on novelty, surprise, and the unexpected jolt of waking up. And because this grasp for control clings to an impossible goal, it becomes yet another source of delusion and suffering.

While that desire for control is part of the meaning of adulthood, and in most ways admirable, it is also one way that we allow accumulating anxieties to block open awareness of reality. No one in attendance at

Vimalakirti's home that day would have supposed that the goddess's dharma proficiency had come to her without extensive practice and serious discipline. Nevertheless, what they got to witness and to realize was that there is always tension in the bodhisattva's life between two kinds of freedom, the freedom that comes from mental discipline and the freedom of letting go. Ideally a balance can be achieved between these skills, between the ability to plan or shape the world and the ability to let the world be whatever it is. This balance is probably best conceived not just as a matter of proportion—how much of each—but also as a matter of timing, a sense of when to buckle down in strenuous effort and when to release that tight grip.

Wherever serious discipline becomes an anxious, joyless struggle, as it appears to be in the sutra's caricature of Śāriputra, there the balanced tension between the freedom of shaping things to be the way we want them to be and the freedom of letting things be whatever they are on their own has given way to one-sided dominance. In the lives of many admirable people, we can see how both of these capacities have been cultivated into alignment. The ability to take control of oneself can be cultivated in tandem with the ability to let oneself go into larger currents of the world.

Those skilled at letting go, releasing the grip of control that they have already achieved, are occasionally given a ride on something much larger, something not in their control that breaks through ordinary boundaries of reality into the new and unforeseen. In that state they get to taste the joys of creative emergence, of innovation. The goddess appears to have been riding just such a wave when she articulated perfectly Buddhist insights about gender identity that nobody had ever imagined before. And here we are two millennia later hoping to be ready to ride waves like that when the next one approaches our lives, hoping, at least, not to be rigidly holding back to conserve something whose time has come and now gone.

Neither Possessed nor Possessing

While maintaining full participation in her practice of the dharma, the goddess has liberated herself from certain restrictions or boundaries

THE GODDESS OF FREEDOM   125

that had been unconsciously imposed on her by the social traditions into which Buddhism had been incorporated. Overcoming long-standing patriarchal gender constraints, she refuses to submit to control and sets herself free. Exuding courage and confidence, and speaking freely, the goddess renounces dogmatic assumptions that had imposed strict limits on what she could think, say, do, and achieve. In doing so, she awakens to a new kind of life. She now stands confidently beyond the gendered boundaries that everyone had falsely assumed to be necessary limits imposed by the true and permanent nature of reality.

But her generous assistance to Śāriputra and to everyone else in at-tendance that day shows another important sense in which the god-dess has abandoned the restrictions of possession and control. Beyond her rebellion against the possessive control of patriarchal constraint, she practices a commitment not to be restrictive or possessive of the mental space in which others need to live. Aware that one form of ownership or rule can be quickly replaced by yet another form—her own form of domination—she teaches Śāriputra the skills of release that had worked so well to set her free. The goddess shows us that this insight of freedom is not just a policy of resistance to forces that con-strain us. It is also a way for all of us to be that extends freedom to others. It is a way to live "free of the habitual notion of possession" (25).

The sutra presents the goddess to us as someone neither possessed nor possessing. She practices the freedom to set out on her own ver-sion of the Buddhist path. She realizes that "the Buddhist path" exists primarily in outline, a set of evolving practices and ways to conceive of life that need to be filled out in concrete detail in each and every unique life. Sutras like the *Vimalakīrti* provide numerous models of the path, different ways that practitioners have taken up the dharma and lived it to guide their own lives. Like others before her, the goddess is an explorer, stretching the dharma into new territories, opening up a full range of practices to suit the diversity of her own life, some of which, she hopes, might inspire further exploration in other lives and in other contexts.

The *Vimalakīrti Sūtra* provides an excellent model of this diversity. Dozens of different practitioners get their turn as characters in the story to say what the Buddhist dharma has come to mean for them.

No one assumes that there is a standard list of possibilities within which everyone must fit. No one insists that there is an exhaustive set of preordained models for Buddhist life to which everyone must conform. This freedom for personal exploration is the context in which the goddess has been able to see and say what no one before her had seen or said. The practice of *pāramitā*—of ongoing self-overcoming— empowers creative ways of envisioning one's own life. It enables innovation—the agility and flexibility to work with an open mind within and around the always changing culture of constraints and possibilities that shape the way life is lived at any point in historical time.

As participants in the modern world, most of us will understand the idea of freedom that we have been discussing in terms of individual autonomy, the personal sovereignty to create our own paths in life. While working with something like that same idea, the *Vimalakīrti Sūtra* would have been simultaneously stretching the scope of freedom in another direction. Aware that exclusive focus on fine-tuning one's own life choices can culminate in a narrowing, delimiting experience of awakening, the sutra keeps pressing on the relation between the freedom that it advocates and the bodhisattva vow to care as much about everyone's spiritual health as their own. The danger of narcissistic focus on personal self-improvement or on enlightenment for oneself was always there in the mind of the author.

So every time the significance of freedom comes up for discussion, the individuality of that idea is soon thereafter decentered by bodhisattvas reimagining what it means to wake up and how that awakening extends the scope of responsibility. All of the different advocates of freedom—the Buddha, Vimalakirti, Mañjuśrī, the goddess—realize that we live, practice, and wake up within particular contexts. We are all situated within what the sutra calls "buddha-fields," settings with particular kinds of people, with particular interests, talents, shortcomings, within particular social, political, economic, religious, and cultural domains. We awaken in the particular ways we do, or fail to do that in the particular ways we fail, together. No one catapults out of their own context to experience possibilities that simply aren't possible in that time and place.

That expansive realization accounts for the importance given in the sutra to the bodhisattva vow. This vow is to keep the relationship between individual concern and communal concern alive and balanced, and not to allow our individual practices to seek the illusory security of personal enclosure. This vow takes into account that, regardless of the extent to which we are loners or joiners, everyone's way of being has a bearing on everyone else's way of being. Not to understand that is to miss one of Vimalakirti's principal insights. Any striving for individual achievement that I take as my achievement, my possession, is based on a misunderstanding, or better, a narrow and limited understanding. The vow expands the range of self-understanding exponentially so that we can see all the ways that our own acts and achievements are integrally linked up with those of others. It enables an awareness of how our own capacity for freedom is always intertwined with the freedom of others.

The bodhisattva vow can also be experienced as a heavy burden. If we take responsibility not just for our own health and well-being but for everyone's, how could it not be? Nevertheless, the experience that the vow offers makes available an expansion and enhancement of freedom, a deeper, more comprehensive sense of liberation. The scope of responsibility that we take upon ourselves shapes the experience of freedom available to us. This is true even if we don't adopt the larger conviction that the bodhisattva vow entails.

Whenever we seek to avoid blame, for example, or make excuses for why we couldn't manage to do what we should have done, thereby denying responsibility, we are at the same time denying our own freedom, denying that it was ever in our power to do whatever we failed to do: "I was prevented from doing it; I was powerless to overcome those obstacles." By narrowing the scope of accountability in order to avoid blame, we narrow and diminish ourselves. "This or that prevented me from getting it done" comes to mean "I'm helpless in the face of this or that, unable to work with obstacles in the way." To the extent that we are unaccountable, we are also unfree, powerless to enact our own intentions. Is avoiding blame really worth forsaking our own freedom?

In adopting the bodhisattva vow, the goddess rebels against this sense of helplessness by expanding the buddha-field or sphere of responsibility in which she acts. She refuses to conceive of herself as powerless, without agency, and by taking responsibility, she also takes that freedom and that power into herself. It is in this sense that contemporary bodhisattvas like Thich Nhat Hanh take responsibility for cultural failures that lead to unnecessary suffering such as homelessness, war, and violence of all kinds. He doesn't just blame others or the government, although they certainly deserve it. It is, he claims, part of his own failure to extend and refine his outreach to others, to bring sensitivity and accountability to others and to the government. And it is his own failure—so far—to transform the hearts and minds of those whose actions perpetuate violence and suffering. If "we" have allowed it to continue, then, from the perspective of the vow, the bodhisattva has also allowed it, regardless of the virtue of his or her own personal efforts.

In facing hardship, suffering, sickness, or death, if we consider ourselves to be alone, we weaken the depth of our response. But in taking that solitary posture, we also fail to consider how our responses to these difficulties will have a profound effect on those around us— our families, children, friends, neighbors, and communities. Realizing this poses a question to us: Can we generate courageous depth and integrity in our response to hardship not just for ourselves but *for their sake*? Can we inspire them by shining a small light of courage and kindness when things get tough? Can we muster the freedom to take responsibility not just to see our own way through but also to serve as guides for those around us when the chips are finally down? Access to that kind of freedom has to be earned in advance. The conditions making courage and freedom possible need to be developed now. But through the practices of self-overcoming, those enabling conditions of freedom just might be there, etched into our character, the next time difficulties and suffering rise up to shake the foundations of our lives. The inevitable question to us is: Who will we be when that time arrives?

What Vimalakirti Couldn't Quite Imagine

At the end of the goddess chapter, Vimalakirti reappears to bring the transformative dialogue between Śāriputra and the goddess to conclusion. Vimalakirti senses that Śāriputra has begun to absorb the goddess's teachings. So Vimalakirti tells the monk more about the goddess, all the amazing places she has been and all the Buddhas she has served. He says finally that "she has truly succeeded in all her vows.... She can live wherever she wishes on the strength of her vow to develop living beings" (63).

Her bodhisattva vow has a "strength," it says, that empowers her to live anywhere she chooses. The vow is to live unselfishly, as though the well-being of others is just as vital as her own—to actually live that way. A more difficult vow could hardly be imagined. But notice that the passage doesn't say that living in that deep state of unselfishness requires a great deal of strength, although we know that it certainly does. It says instead that the vow provides the strength to live in so unselfcentered a way that she could reside anywhere, in any community, under any set of circumstances. According to this, the effort to live the vow doesn't deplete your strength. On the contrary, it generates the required strength within you. The vow is a commitment to self-overcoming, and for those who are willing to take it, the gift it returns is as powerfully enabling as it is unexpected.

If we are historically astute, we might imagine that the author or authors of the *Vimalakīrti Sūtra* would have been somewhat surprised at what we have made of their creation—the goddess. Surprised, because if we had to make an educated guess about the identity of the sutra's author, we would be forced by historical precedent to assume that it was a well-educated, well-positioned monk or several of them. But not a woman. We don't know that, of course, but no matter what the sutra has said, it is highly unlikely that we are listening to a woman's voice given how few women had the opportunity to participate in the literary arts. Thanks to recent research, we now know that there are exceptions to this rule, liberating poems in the *Therīgāthā* by early Buddhist nuns being one of them. But as far as we know, men wrote sutras. On that assumption, let us consider what the creation of the goddess character entailed.

The goddess clearly bests the revered monk in debate over the dharma. She points out Śāriputra's misunderstanding, or the shallow character of the views attributed to him, and in doing that, she discloses a deeper sense of the dharma. She bails him out of logical impasses, but still in each case he can't quite keep up with her. Perhaps we are expected to assume that Vimalakirti could have held his own with her—we don't know—but the author restricts her dialogue to a monk disciple of the purported "lesser vehicle." What we haven't addressed so far, though, is that this formidable bodhisattva is a goddess. She is not a nun, not a woman, not human, even though she adopts a human form to enter the discussion at Vimalakirti's house that day. Being a goddess wouldn't have given her transcendent god-like omnipotence in Indian mythology at that time, but it did mean having somewhat greater power than most human beings.

Making her a goddess—a female deity rather than a male anything—was a norm-breaking gesture for the monk-author of the sutra, even though it was primarily meant to double the embarrassment that Śāriputra would have to endure from the newly emerging Mahayana perspective. But what the author could not do, apparently, was just to make this character a woman. She could have been the matriarch of Vimalakirti's house, or the housekeeper, or a teacher in the local school, or a nun. The goddess's level of brilliance in the dharma, we have to assume, could not be extended to a human being who happened to be female. If the crucial character in the story happens to be female, and if her understanding of the dharma far surpasses that of one of the Buddha's principal disciples, then, apparently, she has to be given some level of divine status because, according to the patriarchal consensus at that time, women just can't do that.

Given that no other author at that time, nor centuries before or after, chose to make that radical move of featuring a woman's brilliance in the dharma over men's, we have to assume that even though the author could picture a female deity in that role, he just wasn't ready to push that theme further by making her human. The theme was there, amazingly enough, but it simply didn't get worked through to its revolutionary potential. But for complex historical reasons, that possibility is a gift that we have received from our recent forebearers, and if we were rewriting this sutra today, we would want this character in the story to be not a goddess but, following through on the sutra's lead, a transgender woman whose skillful means as a teacher fearlessly breaks new ground by showing us that what the Buddha said was true: "In all things, there is neither male nor female" (62). And as long as we're reimagining how the sutra might have taken an alternative course, let's make Vimalakirti one of the goddess's female associates, a highly skilled businessperson and civic leader whose dharma explorations both unnerve and liberate us.

We are free to make moves that don't appear to have been imaginable in the early centuries of Buddhism, no matter how awakened these practitioners might have been. Freedoms evolve. They arise dependent upon conditions. And they disappear in that same way. Two millennia ago the authors of the *Vimalakīrti Sūtra* dropped a hint, a meme, a cultural possibility that even the authors themselves couldn't quite bring to fruition. That hint just sat there hibernating for all those centuries. Then, when complex historical circumstances gave rise to human beings like us, that long-buried hint seems to leap off the page, immediately capturing our attention. Of course she's a woman, a transgender woman, since the moves she makes take her literally "beyond gender." And from that point onward, the groundbreaking insight that only she could articulate opens up whole new vistas for future practitioners of the dharma. The goddess of freedom has been reborn in our time and place to help wake us up.

8

The Dharma of Non-duality

By far the best-known chapter in the *Vimalakīrti Sūtra*—and clearly
the climax of the book—is the ninth chapter, "The Dharma-Door of
Nonduality." Many of the sutra's most provocative statements emerge in
this rapid-paced exchange between the most prominent bodhisattvas
visiting Vimalakirti's residence that day. The chapter opens with a challenge issued by their host. Vimalakirti calls upon each of them to "explain how bodhisattvas enter the dharma-door of nonduality" (73).
One by one, thirty-two bodhisattvas take their best shot at articulating
the highest level of Buddhist wisdom—the vision of comprehensive in-
terfusion between all of the seemingly disparate elements of reality.

Each of their statements is brief and right on the point of the challenge. No one responds to any of these statements, including Mañjuśrī,
who, as the bodhisattva of wisdom, gets to make what would have been
the final statement. Having explained his view, though, Mañjuśrī turns
the challenge back on their host, and the chapter comes to completion in what has long been called Vimalakirti's "thunderous silence."
Evoking non-duality by silently refusing to make any distinction at
all—neither affirmation nor denial—Vimalakirti provides one of the
most famous statements of the dharma in Buddhist history. The earth-
rattling "thunder" of that act of silence still resonates today. But to
set the stage for that climactic event, the bodhisattvas bring different
kinds of dualism to our attention, proposing a variety of ways to experience the all-encompassing non-duality behind the world's many
dichotomies. Let's look at what "dualism" had come to mean and how
the bodhisattvas envision overcoming the divisions that fracture and
divide reality.

Living Skillfully. Dale S. Wright, Oxford University Press. © Oxford University Press 2021.
DOI: 10.1093/oso/9780197587355.003.0009

THE DHARMA OF NON-DUALITY   133

Self and Others: Vowing Non-duality

It would be difficult to count the number of times in the sutra that
Vimalakirti addresses the basic duality between oneself and other
living beings. That had been the focus of his own self-overcoming.
Instead of developing wealth on behalf of himself and his family, he
sought to become the "benefactor of all living beings" (38). He hoped
to "serve as a bridge and ladder for everyone" to free themselves from
the destructive habits of "I" and "mine," and he sought this on behalf
of all living beings rather than as a path to his own awakening (64).
And as Vimalakirti gradually overcame the isolating duality of his own
narrow self-understanding, he began to "recognize in his own suffering the suffering of everyone" (45). For that reason he could eventually say that "his sickness would last just as long as the sickness of
all living beings" since he no longer experienced the divide between
himself and others as insurmountable and final (42). In this way, the
Buddhist teachings of no-self appear everywhere throughout the sutra
as a skillful means of entrance into the non-duality of self and others.

Having heard Vimalakirti's teachings on this dimension of no-self,
several of the bodhisattvas who responded to his challenge choose
this duality to feature in their own statement on entering non-duality.
One of them said: "Dualism is produced from obsession with self, but
true understanding of self does not result in dualism" (76). A "true understanding of self" doesn't leave any room for "obsession with self."
A true understanding of self is attuned to all the ways that the distinct
character of each individual self "arises dependent" upon powerful
influences out beyond the self—culture, history, genetics, economic
circumstances, political pressures, upbringing, neighbors, teachers,
lovers, rivals, and friends. A true understanding of self cannot be
approached without recognition of the permeability and fluidity of the
thin boundaries that separate us. But to arrive at this more comprehensive understanding requires intentional probing and meditative focus.
Until that occurs, we are all dualists, thinking of ourselves—our own-
being—in isolation from all the factors and all the people that have
made us who we are.

Vimalakirti recommends the bodhisattva vow as a way to get over
this shallow self-understanding. But even getting to the point where

we could seriously consider taking a vow to care as much about the well-being of others as we already do about ourselves requires disciplined meditative engagement with deeply entrenched habits of self-absorption. This "obsession with self" is perfectly natural. We all live out of some version of it. The vow is a dharma commitment to cultivate a deeper self-understanding by exposing the self-centered illusions that we have been internalizing from childhood on. The difficulty of this task should not be underestimated. Nor should its promise. The bodhisattva vow offers a liberating form of freedom that arises from a disciplined overcoming of toxic self-obsessions that are grounded in illusions.

Another bodhisattva offers this entry into non-duality: "The dedication of generosity for the sake of attaining enlightenment is dualistic. The nature of generosity is itself enlightenment" (75). Generosity is one of the six paths of self-overcoming, the *pāramitās*. To get past our self-absorbed illusions and to awaken to deeper forms of self-understanding, we can train ourselves to be generous by learning open-hearted giving as a practice. But as this bodhisattva explains, that way of going about it—while initially inevitable—is still dualistic. It still engages in generosity for ulterior motives—our own enlightenment—rather than simply for the well-being of the recipient. Properly understood, he says, "the nature of generosity is itself enlightenment," because that's what it means to awaken from self-absorption—to give unselfishly just because someone is in need. Although compassion and selflessness may begin as a personal project—an impressive achievement of mature selfhood—they never come to final fruition that way.

Another bodhisattva says that " 'I' and 'mine' are two. If there is no presumption of a self, there will be no possessiveness. Thus the absence of presumption is the entrance to nonduality" (73). The possessiveness of our constant concern for what is "mine" shows the pull of duality in the way we conceive of ourselves. If, as this bodhisattva says, we don't presume to be an isolated entity focused on self-protection, then the possessiveness that we're all practicing would have no basis. Losing that basis, we quite naturally let go of emotional attachment to what is "mine." The ideal had been stated earlier in the sutra: "to be responsible for all things yet free of any possessive notion of anything" (27), to get "free of the habits of 'I' and 'mine' " (32). This ideal, grounded in the bodhisattva vow, makes clear that we do not break through our "obsessions of self" by withdrawing from involvements with others in the world. Instead we enter the non-duality of selfhood *through* our engagements with others.

Finally, another bodhisattva offers this: "Self and selflessness are dualistic. Since the existence of self cannot be perceived, what is there to be made selfless?" (74). Doctrinal concerns over whether there is a self or whether there is no self can miss the point of Buddhist practice entirely. Only a truly impressive self could live the vow of selflessness with the kind of depth shown in this sutra and others. What is at stake in Buddhist selflessness is not the abandonment of any part of oneself. It is instead an enlargement and deepening of perspective that extends beyond our deluded ways of relating to ourselves, to others, and to the world. This transformation of perspective overcomes divisive dualities in our minds and functions skillfully to "bring living beings together" (36).

The Non-duality of Purity and Defilement

All traditional religions, Buddhism included, depend in various ways on a careful separation between the pure aspects of life and those that defile people through impurity (or between this impure world and another world of perfect purity beyond it). But in this chapter, several bodhisattvas speak against that traditional duality. One says: " 'Defilement' and 'purification' are two. When there is thorough knowledge of defilement, there will be no conceit about purification. The path leading to complete conquest of all conceit is the entrance into nonduality" (73). The aspiration to purity is a "conceit" that prevents our recognizing our own human finitude. We all experience distraction, possessiveness, self-righteousness, resentment, and on and on, and not to acknowledge that complicity in the world of suffering is to allow delusion to reign. For that reason, a startling statement had already been made in the sutra to the effect that "only those guilty of the five deadly sins can conceive the spirit of enlightenment and attain Buddhahood" (66). This is simply to say that only human beings can conceive the "thought of enlightenment," *bodhicitta*, and awaken from life's most destructive delusions because only human beings dwell in these delusions. There are no grounds for the conceit of purity, nor for arrogant disdain for impurity. Vimalakirti's life story illustrates this point with precision. Although a bodhisattva at the highest level, he ignores the distinction between "pure" and "impure" things, people, and places in his daily life. Vimalakirti is out on street corners talking to everyone, the disciplined citizens of elevated status and the undisciplined people of ill repute. He shows up in bars and casinos, traditionally "impure" places where no respectable Buddhist would have gone. Buddhists had thought that these places threaten one's prospects for awakening, and that would certainly be true if "awakening" is conceived as individual purity of mind. But that's exactly why Vimalakirti is out there in the "impure" world. Awakening isn't just about him. It's for all of us equally. So Vimalakirti's practice doesn't focus on protecting his spiritual purity. In fact, if he did orient his practice that way he would have undermined his own "thought of enlightenment." With the conviction of *bodhicitta* and a commitment to the bodhisattva vow, Vimalakirti is able to go anywhere and be with anyone, wherever suffering is a basic human issue. Everywhere.

A second bodhisattva says: "To say, 'this is impure' and 'this is immaculate' makes for duality. One who, attaining equanimity, forms no concepts of impurity or immaculateness yet is not utterly without conception . . . enters the absence of conceptual knots, thus entering nonduality" (74). Dualistic concepts that isolate the pure from the impure just don't fit the world in which we live, where everything is mixed, entangled, and influenced by their opposites. Authentic understanding of the reality in which we live requires that these stark dichotomies be undermined by the complexities that "dependent arising" will always bring into play. For that reason, this bodhisattva doesn't "form" these mental dualisms. "Yet," it says, one is "not utterly without conception." To be without conception is to be incapable of thinking, and thinking is precisely what this bodhisattva is doing—thinking at a far deeper and more inclusive level than stark conceptual dichotomies allow. Finally, it says that the ability to "empty" these dualistic conceptions untangles the "conceptual knots" that obstruct clarity of mind and skillful action.

Another bodhisattva addresses Vimalakirti's challenge by saying: "It is dualistic to detest the world and to rejoice in liberation. Neither detesting the world nor rejoicing in liberation is nonduality. Why? Liberation can be found where there is bondage, but where there is no bondage there is no need for liberation. To be neither bound nor liberated is to enter nonduality" (76). All of us quite naturally detest the impure world of cruelty and suffering and rejoice in the prospects of liberation from this world. The world is radically distorted—politically, socially, economically, religiously—and therefore prone to suffering at almost unimaginable levels. But that fact is precisely Vimalakirti's reason for committing himself fully to it, his reason for practicing complete allegiance to ordinary people, all of us who reside here. That people are homeless or addicted, that they haven't bathed in weeks, that there are children malnourished while others hoard food and wealth, that crime destroys lives on a daily basis—this is precisely the reason to dwell on this world, not the occasion to turn away from it in dualistic rejection.

Therefore, Vimalakirti is imagined to practice a fully inclusive social world, and to practice a spiritual life that is riveted on all dimensions of this life and this world. His highest aspiration is to wake up in this world, not from it. He practices on behalf of this world, and he will not forsake it because he has seen through the delusional dichotomy between the pure and the impure. So, in a poem that Vimalakirti had recited to the gathering, he says that "true bodhisattvas . . . never dwell upon the least difference between the Buddha and themselves" (68), even though they serve the Buddha and take refuge in the Buddha. The stark distinction between Buddha and non-Buddha, like that between purity and impurity, is exposed as a delusion that distorts the reality in which we are enveloped.

This is the same reason that Vimalakirti had given to the monks gathered around the Buddha for why "you should enter the homes of ordinary people as if entering the family of the Buddha" (26). It is also why Vimalakirti explains that the "miserable," "demanding beggars" that you encounter on the street are in fact awakened bodhisattvas, "who through their skill-in-means, wish to test the 'firm resolve'" of the bodhisattvas' commitment to their vow (55). This, of course, is less a statement of fact than it is an awakened challenge: Can we learn to treat all people as we would treat the Buddha? Can we learn to treat the Buddha as we would all people so that the liberating entrance into mindful non-duality is actualized not elsewhere but right here in the life of our global community?

Non-duality Between the Human and the Non-human

Not even one of the thirty-two bodhisattvas responding to Vimalakirti's challenge to address non-duality spoke about the duality that we today feel so strongly between the human and the non-human natural world. No one had anything to say about the non-duality of the biosphere—the necessary interdependence between all life-forms on earth. Nor did anyone address the non-duality and integrity of the cosmos as a whole. That's interesting. Why not? Why wouldn't any of these awakened bodhisattvas respond to Vimalakirti by pointing out the interconnections between human beings and all other living beings? Why didn't any of them try to articulate how the organic and inorganic dimensions of reality constitute a non-dual whole?

Could it be that no one living in India two thousand years ago—or anywhere else in the world for that matter—would have felt the kinds of estrangement from the natural world that we feel today? If you don't sense a problem, you don't seek a solution—you don't even bring it up. Although the northern Indian plains were already undergoing rapid urbanization at that time, a sense of alienation from the natural world was hardly a problem. Even city dwellers lived in the natural world to an extent that we can't even imagine. Differentiation from the natural world was more likely what they sought, as was true in other axial-age civilizations. If there were "back to nature" enthusiasts in India then they would probably have evoked more puzzlement or derision than a serious following. Like everyone else in the world at that time, Indian culture was headed irretrievably forward into this duality rather than back out of it.

Recall the extent to which the Indian concept of the zoological sphere at that time was already more thoroughly non-dual than anything to be found in Western cultures. Even before Buddhism, the idea was circulating that all "living beings" or all "sentient beings" were linked together through the incessant processes of reincarnation. "Human being" was just one kind of being in the larger hierarchy of all living beings. All forms of conscious life were interlinked, they thought, and individual beings moved up, down, or sideways through the many destinies offered by the zoosphere as they had done forever. So although it could have occurred to the sutra's author to have one of the thirty-two respondents point out the non-duality of all living beings, it simply didn't come up. It could have come up, since the bodhisattva vow is to awaken literally all sentient beings. But the issue targeted in the vow was the compassion necessary to strive toward that expanded thought of enlightenment, rather than the question of whether all living beings were in fact interconnected. They agreed on the latter while riveted on the former—how to unleash the motivation of awakening for all.

As a result of those factors and no doubt many more, the non-duality of the biosphere or the cosmos as a whole was never mentioned in Vimalakirti's quest to illuminate the deepest meaning of non-duality. Why does it occur to us? Presumably because our current ecological crisis makes it suddenly crucial, and because literally all developments in biological science and all of the other sciences point to non-duality. Earlier Western culture had been much more heavily dualized than Indian culture—the duality between human beings and other beings was categorically stark. Even if all living beings had been created by the same Creator God, the biblical status given to human beings created in the image of God differentiated us so thoroughly that few writers ever discussed our similarities to other animals or our interconnections. Prior to Darwin, earthly life was thought to have been entirely about human beings, created for us and us alone.

As evolutionary biology developed, we began to see ourselves as one among millions of species, indeed as one of the latest arrivals. Although there has been strenuous resistance, as the ecological sciences developed alongside evolutionary biology we have come to accept the fundamental interdependence of all forms of life, at least in principle, if not yet in our daily practices. This much more expansive view of the totality of life constitutes a major change of worldview in Western cultures, and the best way to characterize the newly emerging vision is the non-duality of the overarching biosphere. We are recognizing the non-duality of life in ways that have never surfaced before anywhere in the world, and this development is taking place globally. In celebration of this important transformation of vision, and in an effort to push it further, let us take Vimalakirti's challenge upon ourselves. Joining the many bodhisattvas providing responses to the question of non-duality that day, what dimensions of the truth of non-duality might we be able to contribute to the sutra's list?

- Non-duality between levels of human population/consumption and the degree/speed of climate change
- Non-duality between the expansion of human population/consumption and the extinction of millions of species
- Non-duality between our capacities to restrain human population/consumption and the quality of life for all species on the planet
- Non-duality between our use of fossil fuels and the temperature of the earth
- Non-duality between human emissions of various kinds and the quality of the planet's breathable atmosphere
- Non-duality between my own personal carbon footprint and the effects of over-carbonization on all living beings
- Non-duality between the purity of our water supplies and the health of our communities
- Non-duality between the direct effects of wars and the indirect effects felt by all living beings on earth
- Non-duality through evolution between single-cell life-forms and the most highly developed forms of human consciousness
- Non-duality between life and death that constitutes the living processes of the biosphere
- Non-duality between myself as an agent within the network of networks and all other beings in the cosmos
- Non-duality between our own human well-being and the well-being of all other beings in the biosphere as a whole
- Finally, to restate one of Vimalakirti's own: non-duality between wisdom as the capacity to align ourselves with reality and compassion as the felt recognition that all living beings are in this together

Beyond this short list, you could add many more. If the distinguishable elements of reality are, for all practical purposes, infinite, this list would also go forward endlessly. If all things really are intertwined with all other things, the Buddhist concept of "dependent arising," having gone through innumerable twists and turns of evolution, continues to function at the very center of the teachings. This teaching points directly at a set of serious challenges for us. Can we achieve the level of understanding and wisdom that would motivate us to profoundly alter our habitual ways of living so that the biosphere that constitutes life on our planet can be mindfully maintained? Can we collectively transform our global self-understanding so that we instinctually nurture the entire organic order, the comprehensive network of life now seemingly in our charge and without which human life ends? Can we learn to conceive of ourselves in this way, as charged with the responsibility of maintaining the earth and all of its biodiversity? Can we achieve a unified vision of our human place within the natural world that gives us a deep sense of connectedness to the earth as a whole? Can we generate cooperation and a sense of solidarity among human beings that is global and all-inclusive? Can we undergo a transformation of self-understanding far-reaching enough not just to envision but most importantly to live skillfully within the paradigm-shattering truths of non-duality?

Open Inclusivity: Non-duality Between Us and Them

There is one persistent duality that runs throughout the *Vimalakīrti Sūtra*, that between Mahayana Buddhists like the author and other Buddhists who are regarded as practitioners of a "lesser vehicle." Some passages disparage or humor the "disciples," those who were later dismissively called "Hinayana" Buddhists. In other passages they appear as foils for bodhisattvas like Vimalakirti whose wisdom can be featured in contrast. Although none of these passages amount to full-scale condemnation, the dichotomy between "us" and "them" is noticeable even if these different Buddhists are pictured as practicing together under the tutelage of the same Buddha.

In response to Vimalakirti's challenge, however, one bodhisattva rises to the occasion by acknowledging the "Hinayana/Mahayana" duality and showing the importance of transcending it. Here is how it reads: "The bodhisattva Subāhu declared, 'bodhisattva-spirit' and 'disciple-spirit' are two. When both are seen to resemble an illusory spirit, there is no bodhisattva-spirit and disciple-spirit. Thus, the sameness of natures of spirits is the entrance into nonduality" (73). "Bodhisattvas" and "disciples" represent the two kinds of practitioners featured throughout the sutra. They are clearly distinct in the author's mind since the superiority of one over the other is repeatedly featured. Yet in this crucial chapter the author is nevertheless able to have one bodhisattva admit that these are empty categories, that both kinds of Buddhism are empty of static own-being. This would mean that both sets of practitioners and the distinctions between them are impermanent, always open to revision, and that they become what they are at any given point in time dependent on particular historical, social, and cultural conditions. In the sutra's terms, whatever it is that appears to separate the "bodhisattvas" from the "disciples" is empty of own-being. Such dualities should not be allowed to harden into an ongoing dogma. They cannot be given priority over the bodhisattva vow to extend the open arms of mindful understanding and compassion to all living beings.

Probably not on the exact same point, but along similar lines of realization, another bodhisattva seeks to overcome dualism by declaring that "it is dualistic to speak of good paths and bad paths. One who is on the path is not concerned with good or bad paths. . . . Understanding the nature of concepts, his mind does not engage in duality. Such is the entrance into nonduality" (76). Those reading this sutra in traditional Buddhist cultures would no doubt have taken their own Mahayana vehicle to be the good path and the disciples' vehicle to be not necessarily "bad" but at least less good.

Similarly, but likely with more disdain, they would probably have conceived of the difference between Buddhism as a whole and other traditions being practiced in their cultural world as a difference between good and bad paths. This passage, however, seems to say that once you're seriously engaged in a practice of awakening— self-overcoming through generosity, tolerance, and wisdom, for

example—you're neither congratulating yourself on your own good-
ness nor condemning others since the practice should have liberated you from that self-centered and judgmental posture. It says that
through "understanding the nature of concepts"—their tendency to
bifurcate and to divide everything into untenable categories of "us"
and "them"—the bodhisattva's mind doesn't settle into the divisive
illusions they tend to encourage.

Other passages warn against clinging to hardened dichotomies between similar pairs—good and evil, true and false, sinless and sinful.
This is not and certainly cannot be an admonition not to form such
concepts, not to make such distinctions at all. We've already heard
one bodhisattva explain that overcoming dualism doesn't leave you
"without conceptions" (74). You can't live a human life without them.
The distinction between good idea and bad idea, between poisonous
food and nourishing food, or between worthwhile and worthless
practice is crucial. Cultivating *bodhicitta*, developing an aspiration
to awakening, requires choosing the teachings and practices that will
constitute your path while forgoing others. You've got to make some
serious judgments. The point of these evocations of non-duality is
not to surrender the freedom to decide and choose but rather to practice freedom from debilitating dogmatism and hardened patterns of
thought that confine and divide everything irrevocably. Their point is
the freedom to understand more comprehensively, more insightfully,
and more flexibly.

Hardened, inflexible, and habitual categories are severely divisive.
They obscure the open, always changing, and relational character of
mind and reality. In the culture of our time the impropriety and injustice of other long-standing dualities have come forcefully to our
attention—those between different racial and ethnic groups, different
linguistic groups, different socioeconomic classes, different sexual
orientations, different abilities and ages. In all of these ways and others,
we have sought to break through static dualism, however unsuccess-
fully so far. The damage to individual lives from hardened gender
dualism is one of the primary issues of our time, even though we've
already seen how it was featured two thousand years ago as one theme
in the *Vimalakīrti Sūtra*.

One form of dualism appearing throughout the *Vimalakīrti Sūtra* derives from a challenging irony at the heart of the concept of the Mahayana, the vehicle "great" or "comprehensive" enough to include everyone. Whenever the Mahayana vow or intention to encompass "all living beings" leads to a harsh condemnation of those who refuse to accept this as the highest goal in life, the Mahayana has become just another divisive category, yet another duality to add to the list separating "us" from "them." To overcome their own dualism, Mahayana Buddhists would have to commit themselves to social and cultural inclusivity in all conceivable forms. They would need to avoid the kinds of exclusivism and religious nationalism that have recently overwhelmed all of the world's religions. Each of these traditions struggle in their own unique ways with delusions that derive from the "us" versus "them" mentality.

Opting for a posture of non-dualistic inclusivity, Buddhists would commit themselves to working with our shared humanity. They would commit to working through cultural conflicts and disagreements peacefully and cooperatively based on a vow to identify and pursue the common good for all living beings. Although reactions against the rapidly unfolding globalism are inevitable, sometimes justifiable, the truth of the unity of humanity and the non-duality of the biosphere must eventually outweigh all other factors. Inclusivity—a patient, open non-dualism—is the "Mahayana" of our time in history.

It is important to recognize, however, that this principle of inclusivity—the universality of the vow to care for the well-being of all living beings—is too general to function on its own at the level of everyday practice. It needs to be complemented by skillful means of carrying it forward because differences between individuals, groups, cultures, ages, genders, and ethnicities are real and binding, even if open and changing. They must be given full consideration in determining how we will treat different people. The universal vow to care about everyone doesn't tell us in detail how to work with anyone. Individuals are different and these differences require skillful, nuanced attention.

It is also true that we have many different kinds of relationships. We can't treat other people's children as if they were our own, just as it is crucial to treat intimates in our own life very differently from the ways we treat everyone else. Although everybody counts and everybody deserves our mindful consideration, in the domain of everyday life and direct responsibilities, skillfully applied differences need to guide our relationships. Nobody needs to be patronized by aggressive, controlling "generosity," no matter how well-meaning. Love and compassion extended out to people we don't know will often best take the form of justice, tolerance, and intercultural sensitivity. These qualifications don't invalidate the universal vow to care about all living beings. They just give it the skillful means to function on the ground where we always stand, while continually striving to overcome our limitations in order to reach out further and more inclusively with wisdom and compassion.

From Non-dual Vision to Vimalakirti's Silence

An alternative title for the *Vimalakīrti Sūtra* as a whole was "The Sutra on the Reconciliation of Dualities." The sutra describes Vimalakirti as the foremost practitioner of non-duality, as someone whose vision of the comprehensive whole encompasses all of the diverse aspects of the world and brings them to reconciliation. But the reconciliation of dualities or differences is not their obliteration. Vimalakirti doesn't just see the undifferentiated unity of all things. He sees how all things come together to form the current totality while still being as distinct from each other as before. He sees the difference between rich and poor with great clarity and works to change it. He sees the difference between those who suffer horribly and those who do not, the difference between those who face difficulties with skill and composure and those who do not. All of these differences still stand. Non-dualism is not monism.

This is to say that the world Vimalakirti experiences is just as complex, messy, confusing, and fast-moving as anyone else's world. Vimalakirti's practice, then, is not to create a world without differences of opinion, without tension or conflict; such a world would be lifeless, without movement and complexity. His practice is to find all of this interesting, to be mindful enough in apprehending this complexity to see what is really going on while not losing his bearings or his patience in facing it.

Vimalakirti is pictured as someone who is not unnerved and thrown off balance when tensions rise or when different standpoints challenge one another. He appears to have overcome the discomfort that we all feel in situations that are tense and complicated. He has cultivated composure, flexibility, and resilience and calls upon these skills to lend balance and hope to others. His non-dualism is a working vision, an experienced understanding of the whole that isn't compelled by fear to shut anyone or anything out.

What grounds this kind of composure? What gives it support or backing sufficient to enable such skillful intervention? A profound sense of non-duality. A vision of all the ways that opposition and conflict are essential dimensions of the reality within which we live. Sensing how at some level all of these differences and tensions are working together provides a kind of composed equanimity that makes the skillful work of mediation possible. Realizing how and why very different things have come together makes it possible to work effectively with them.

While most of us struggle with the conflict between our own meditative practice and our concern for the well-being of others, Vimalakirti experiences them working together, their non-duality. He sees that personal transformation is made possible by collective, historical change in the past and present, and that change in the community is often precipitated by individual insight and leadership. Vimalakirti understands how the wisdom or enlightenment of one outstanding individual is the outcome of a "thought of enlightenment" that has developed over long periods of incubation in the larger culture. He gets in a visceral way that any achievement of human excellence that comes to fruition in his life is much, much more than the result of his own effort. It is the product of a collective human effort over long stretches of historical time and of the evolutionary "non-effort" that reaches far back beyond that.

That is why the sutra shows Vimalakirti taking pride in the achievements of ordinary citizens throughout his city. He sees their individual merits as works of art that everyone has produced together. His enlarged vision of non-duality overcomes the illusions of personal self-interest, allowing him to experience "sympathetic joy" whenever anyone rises to the cultural level of greatness. These individuals are, so to speak, collective works of art, small spots of greatness that the community can be proud to have co-produced. This non-dual vision is the result of Vimalakirti's lifelong meditation on the interdependent "emptiness" of all aspects of reality. Nothing is what it is just on its own.

And that includes Vimalakirti himself. He did nothing to create his own life—he was just born, an act of grace. He didn't earn or make the water he drinks nor the air he breathes. He just receives them along with the solar energy that releases the forces of life within and around him. Everything he is and everything he has come to him as gifts from others, from his family, from his teachers, from farmers, from bakers, from nature, from reality itself. He is nothing in and of himself, but lives this gift within the non-dual powers of the larger world.

Vimalakirti has experienced great freedom in his life, but that freedom is not the absence of causal determination. Quite the contrary: determining forces have made his life and his freedom possible. Sensing the vital necessity of both sides of this duality—freedom and causality—Vimalakirti practices a balance between his strenuous effort and surrender, between striving and release of grip, between hard-won achievement and wide-open gratitude. The possessive "his" of "his freedom" has been decentered along with "his self" since this individual self is in truth one small creation in the evolutionary unfolding of the infinitely larger cosmos.

The non-duality that Vimalakirti teaches is just the open-minded, open-hearted awareness of our unlimited connections, a sense of being encompassed and supported by forces all around and far beyond us. These insights give rise to a feeling of gratitude for the gift of our own existence and a natural humility that readily acknowledges our humble position in the vast scope of reality. That non-dual vision is what inspires Vimalakirti's famous silence. Awe, wonder, and gratitude take the words right out of his mouth. Momentarily relieved of all responsibility, Vimalakirti just sits there smiling, all the way down to his marrow.

Conclusion

Silence and the Dharma, Dueling

It would be natural to assume that Vimalakirti's "thunderous silence" would bring the sutra honoring him to a close. That would have been the perfect ending—brilliant, in fact. But it doesn't end there, as several more chapters and an epilogue continue on to eclipse the sounds of silence.

Not only does the sutra go on for a few more chapters, but even the climactic chapter on non-dualism doesn't come to a resounding end in Vimalakirti's gesture of silence. Instead of concluding right there, Mañjuśrī steps forward again to praise the act of silence: "Excellent! Excellent, noble sir," he says. "This is indeed the entrance into the nonduality of the bodhisattvas. Here there is no use for syllables, sounds, and ideas" (77). But clearly there *is* a "use for syllables, sounds, and ideas" or he wouldn't have interrupted the silence in order to speak them. Apparently, Vimalakirti's silence was insufficient to stand on its own. To be noticed and appreciated silence needed to be pointed out and praised. Without those words of clarification, silence might not have meant anything at all, or even worse, it might have been misinterpreted.

Earlier in the sutra, whenever a participant in dialogue fell into silence it was taken to be a sign of failure. On two occasions, Śāriputra is described as having "faltered" by retreating into silence, unable to respond to dharma insight from Vimalakirti in one instance and from the goddess in another. When he opted for silence in response to the goddess, Śāriputra was chided for the dualism embedded in his understanding of the dharma and told that you "can't point to liberation by abandoning speech" (59). In these cases, silence was anything but enlightening. So, when Vimalakirti did what Śāriputra had done—a silent lack of response—there was danger of misunderstanding.

Living Skillfully. Dale S. Wright, Oxford University Press. © Oxford University Press 2021.
DOI: 10.1093/oso/9780197587355.003.0010

Concerned that this speechless vacuum might be misconstrued, taken as an inability or a failure, Mañjuśrī immediately spoke up to make sure that everyone recognized this as a different kind of silence, a "thunderous silence" capable of evoking awareness of non-duality. Because the absence of words might have seemed much the same in both instances, words of explanation were added to guarantee that Vimalakirti's silence could be distinguished from Śāriputra's. This tells us that even if silence had brought the discussion of non-duality to brilliant completion, it accomplished that only when given meaning by Mañjuśrī's non-silent explanation. And the irony of using "syllables, sounds, and ideas" to point out that "there is no use for syllables, sounds, and ideas" slips by everyone without notice, just as the silence itself had disappeared into Mañjuśrī's praise of it.

Nor does the chapter end there with Mañjuśrī's verbal praise of silent non-duality. The sutra's narrator then steps in to make certain that readers get the point, reporting that "when these teachings had been declared, five thousand bodhisattvas entered the door of the dharma of nonduality and attained tolerance for the emptiness of all things" (77). Bodhisattvas entered the dharma-door of non-duality "when these teachings had been declared." The sutra thereby tells us that the "declaration" of these teachings, all thirty-two of them, precipitated the experience of non-duality even if Vimalakirti's own statement—his silence—was the capstone that brought the verbal teachings to their highest point of articulation. In fact, half of the sutra's other chapters end in a similar declaration—that when these teachings were presented a huge number of listeners were awakened. These realizations highlight for us the role that language has played at the heart of the Buddhist dharma, especially its role in relation to the silence of meditation.

As Buddhism evolved through the centuries, the "thunder" of Vimalakirti's silence grew louder and louder. Teachers in various traditions called upon it as a capstone statement to their own versions of the dharma, just as Vimalakirti had done. Early Zen masters throughout East Asia contemplated it, challenged students with it, and taught it as the focal point of meditation. Still echoing centuries later, it was canonized into Zen koan practice, surfacing most notably in case #84 of the *Blue Cliff Record* and as case #48 of the *Book of Equanimity*.

Silence had come to play a crucial role in the dharma, a role that we should consider a significant part of Vimalakirti's legacy. It functioned as an honest disclaimer, as the dharma's own humble self-denial. And as a warning about the dangers of attachment to Buddhism, silence reminded practitioners about unexpected reappearances of ego assertion and dogmatism. It served as a disclaimer to the presumption of closure and finality, the inner urge to cling and repel—remaining vestiges of the first two poisons, greed and hatred. And this same silence functioned to alert practitioners to delusions that eat away at the freedom discovered in the practice of mindfulness.

But the author of the sutra, like the Zen masters who practiced it, knew better than to be silent about silence. They realized that silence could only do its liberating work in close relation to the language of the dharma. They understood that the dualistic separation of language and silence was a trap, a delusion that would fare no better than any other duality. They saw that choosing one side over the other would just deepen the delusion. These explorers of the dharma realized that just like "non-attachment," "letting go," and "emptying," silence couldn't fulfill its liberating function unless it made its appearance within the language of awakening. They realized that what the sutra called "Vimalakirti's eloquence"—his fluency in the dharma—was so intertwined with his non-verbal equanimity that one couldn't exist without the other. So even if silence and the dharma seem to be locked in a duel, it is in the interest of everyone's awakening that neither one wins, neither dies, and that they learn to live and to practice together. That deep and balanced coordination was the secret of Vimalakirti's non-duality.

Epilogue: Final Instructions from the Buddha

The *Vimalakīrti Sūtra* ends with an epilogue, a concluding statement about the overall status of the sutra and how it should be treated in the future. The epilogue begins with divine sanction, when Śakra, "prince of the gods," says to the Buddha that of the "many hundreds of thousands of teachings of the dharma" he's heard, none are as "remarkable" as this one (96). He goes on to claim that if anyone hears "this teaching of the dharma, accepts it, remembers it, reads it and understands it deeply they will be, without a doubt, true vessels of the dharma" (96). He then mentions that "there is no need to mention that those who apply themselves to the yoga of meditation on it" will receive many benefits, including "cutting off all unhappy lives, opening their way to all fortunate lives." They will "overcome all adversaries," "conquer all devils," "be honored by all Buddhas," and much more (96).

Up to this point in the sutra, we hadn't encountered claims of this kind. Everything had been oriented to insight and wisdom and virtually nothing promised good fortune—success, victory, happiness—to those who take up the practice of these teachings. Even the Buddha's several miracles had been staged in the service of wisdom, each one demonstrating a specific point that had to be contemplated and realized. This change in the sutra's tactics can be considered a final twist of *upāya*—skill-in-means for cultivating the dharma through the dissemination of this sutra. The author clearly wants to attract as many readers as possible and to do that puts more than "insight" and "awakening" on offer. If the promise of spiritual insight and awakening is insufficient to lure you into active engagement, how about more tangible rewards like good fortune in worldly matters? After all, having practiced these exact teachings, Vimalakirti, the sutra's hero, had been blessed with an abundance of good fortune. He enjoyed success, power, fame, and riches even though he hadn't sought them.

This is a question about outcomes and expectations. What could someone expect the results of mastery in these meditative disciplines to be? And as we've seen, the answer is left wide open for interpretation, knowing that what motivates people can vary enormously. Rejecting no one, inviting everyone to board the "large vehicle"—the Mahayana—requires great flexibility about points of departure. The author of the *Vimalakīrti Sūtra* had already shown impressive skill for inclusive communication. Although the sutra is filled with rarified, high-level dharma meditations, it also includes miracles, humor, great stories. The *upāya*-savvy strategy was to open it up and provide something for everyone because not everyone will start out on the path with the same goals in mind. Motivations will differ enormously. But the sutra's author clearly knew that whatever practitioners' expectations might be at the outset, the transformative effects of practice alter motivation. Motivating goals that at first might have been attractive and desirable lose their allure, especially as the sense of "I" and "mine" recedes and "the habits of possessiveness" dissipate. Successful practice changes everything, especially motivations.

Having left the question of outcomes and expectations wide open, the sutra then raises a question about what kinds of practice would be most efficacious. Posing a question to Śakra, the Buddha asks: If people were to dedicate their lives to serving many Buddhas, and then when the Buddhas passed away, they built beautiful memorial shrines (stupas) of precious stones, adorning them with "parasols, banners, and lamps," and if they then made offerings at these shrines for many years, showering them with flowers and perfumes, "while playing drums and music," "how much merit would these people have earned as a result of such activities?" (97). Śakra responds with confidence: "Many, many merits. It would be impossible to measure the limit of these merits" (97).

The Buddha then makes his point. He says, "Understand this, Śakra. Whoever accepts the *Vimalakīrti Sūtra*, recites it, and understands it deeply, he or she will gather merits even greater than those who perform the above acts. Why? Because the enlightenment of the Buddhas arises from the dharma, and one honors them by dharma worship, not by material worship. Thus it is taught, prince of gods, and thus you must understand it" (97). The sutra's author doesn't denounce the pious building of shrines and the exuberant practice of devotional rituals. The Buddha appears to accept Śakra's claim that doing these things brings a person "many merits." But praise for those activities in a few sentences at the end of the sutra is greatly overshadowed by the kinds of religious practice featured throughout this text—those that focus on understanding what the sutra has said by disciplined engagement in the dharma through meditative practice. These practices of insight and comprehension earn "even greater" merit than honoring the Buddhas in ritual precisely because "the enlightenment of the Buddhas"—the reason anyone honors them—"arises from the dharma," not the other way around (97).

The next several pages explain this preference for insight meditation over ritual piety and material offerings by elaborating on what it now calls "dharma worship." The sutra asks: "What is this dharma worship?" (*dharmapuja*) (98). *Puja*, here translated as "worship," is a religious ritual of devotion typically directed to a deity—in Buddhism, to the Buddha or Buddhas or to renowned saints and bodhisattvas. *Dharmapuja* or "dharma worship" would therefore be a discipline of devotion directed to the dharma, to Buddhist teachings and practices rather than to deities. And as the epilogue explains it, dharma worship is essentially what has been featured all the way through the sutra.

Dharma worship elevates the practice of the dharma above all else. It seeks to engage the Buddhist teachings by practicing meditation religiously, that is, with single-minded devotion. It pursues insight by meditating on the thought of enlightenment, impermanence, dependent arising, no-self, emptiness, the six perfections, the bodhisattva vow, non-duality, and skillful means, and it seeks to enable the practitioner to embody these teachings in every aspect of life, to encompass them in "body, speech and mind." In the final analysis dharma worship seeks to evoke insight, wisdom, and compassion by overcoming "the habits of 'I' and 'mine' " and "the habit of clinging to an ultimate ground" (99). Dharma worship is training in self-overcoming, and self-overcoming is what empowers Vimalakirti's awakened and skillful life.

Having introduced the ordinary piety of "material worship" as a possibility—building and decorating shrines in order to honor the Buddhas and receive religious merit in return—the Buddha appears to take it back. He says: "Therefore, prince of gods, do not worship me with material objects but worship me with dharma worship. Do not honor me with material objects but honor me by honoring the dharma" (100). To honor the dharma is to make it the focal point of practice in a quest to integrate its wisdom into all aspects of life and, directed by that wisdom, to serve others with skill and compassion.

Two points have been made in the epilogue so far: first, that practice of this sutra leads to good fortune, however that is understood, whether as success in life or as wisdom in life; and second, that even though there are many worthwhile forms of spiritual practice, the best of these and the one sanctioned by the Buddha and bodhisattvas like Vimalakirti is insight meditation that deepens wisdom and compassion. These two points bring the sutra's teaching to a close. From here the author addresses matters of assurance and dedication.

The Buddha turns to Maitreya, the future Buddha, for a final dedication of this sutra to the future: "I transmit to you, Maitreya, this unexcelled, perfect enlightenment . . . in order that this teaching will spread in the world and will not disappear" (100). The Buddha expresses concern that if people in the future don't have the opportunity "to hear this teaching of the dharma" they will be profoundly disadvantaged. In reply, Maitreya pledges himself to the task of disseminating the *Vimalakīrti Sūtra*. He distinguishes between "two gestures of the bodhisattvas," one that simply "believes all sorts of words and phrases" and another that overcomes dualism by penetrating to the heart of the sutra's teachings through meditative practice (101). He admits that there may be some "beginners" who are "terrified and doubtful" when they encounter "this teaching never before heard" (101). But Maitreya commits himself to cultivating the deepest realization of the sutra's meaning.

Maitreya concludes with a promise to the Buddha: "In the future, I will place in the hands of noble sons and noble daughters who are worthy vessels of the holy dharma this profound teaching. I will instill in them the power of memory with which they may, having believed in this teaching, retain it, recite it, penetrate its depths, teach it, propagate it, write it down, and proclaim it extensively to others" (102). The Buddha responds gratefully: "Excellent, excellent! Your word is well given. The Buddha rejoices and commends your good promise" (102).

Finally, then, the Buddha turns to his disciple Ānanda, traditionally credited with having memorized all the Buddha's talks, or sutras, in order to preserve them faithfully and to make them available to all future practitioners. Ānanda's certification was taken to be the sign of authenticity for all sutras as true expressions of the dharma. So, the Buddha instructs Ānanda to "receive the *Vimalakīrti Sūtra* as an expression of the dharma." He asks Ānanda to "remember it and teach it widely and correctly to others." Ānanda assures him: "I have memorized this expression of the teaching of the dharma" (102), thus also assuring future readers like us of the authenticity of the teachings provided in this sutra.

How Should We Read the *Vimalakīrti Sūtra*?

Although the epilogue reasserts some of the sutra's primary themes in innovative ways, it also poses something of a challenge to contemporary Buddhist readers because its expressions of self-promotion can seem to run against the grain of its own teachings. The author of the sutra has the Buddha guarantee the validity and importance of these teachings rather than simply letting them stand or fall on their own merits. And it promises rewards of good fortune to those who dedicate themselves to the propagation of this text without seeming to notice how that promise of reward might contradict the disciplines of selfless non-possessiveness that the sutra had just taught. Why couldn't the sutra have made its exit more gracefully by demonstrating the kinds of self-overcoming that it had been teaching so skillfully?

The sutra's epilogue follows a standard procedure for concluding Mahayana sutras. Virtually all of them engage in some form of self-promotion, from assurances by the Buddha to promises of reward for engaging them in practice. It's not difficult to imagine why authors might have been tempted to end them this way. First of all, these sutras were an entirely new kind of literature in a culture that was just becoming literate at a much higher level. The success that a few of these sutras attained in the long run was far from certain at the outset. Unsurprisingly, authors sought skillful means to encourage their being taken seriously.

Second, though, if we try to imagine what the proliferation of a new text would have required at that time, we can sense the motives for creative tactics. Imagine yourself to have just finished writing a sutra, a long and complicated text, demanding many months or years of hard work. There it is, one copy, vulnerable to everything from the next rainstorm to fire on the kitchen hearth. No backups. All texts and copies were meticulously written by hand on bark or parchment with crude writing instruments. To get even one copy, a second, someone had to be motivated to undertake the enormous task of writing out an exact duplicate by hand.

With some urgency, a new religious practice emerged—meditative writing, mastering the teachings of a sutra by writing a copy, perhaps two. For a text to be exponentially disseminated—to go viral—it had to be potent enough to motivate hundreds of people to devote the many, many weeks or months it would take to produce a legible and accurate copy. For a text of any kind to make it through its first decade, let alone many centuries in many different cultures, something of a minor miracle had to occur. Authors sought to motivate this miracle. From their point of view, the continuance of the dharma was at stake, and this concern was inseparable from their vow as bodhisattvas. Taking all that into consideration helps us understand apparent expressions of self-interest that bring the sutra to a close. It is entirely possible that without these few expressions of self-concern, the *Vimalakīrti Sūtra* would have never survived down through the centuries and into our hands for consideration.

The question that the epilogue raises, especially for us as contemporary readers, concerns the kind of relationship to the sutra that a reader or practitioner should cultivate. What should our purposes be in reading it? What posture in relation to it would be most productive? Although it is vital that we answer these questions on our own, each in our own ways, here is what the sutra advises in the epilogue. The author recommends that we "accept it," "read it," "believe it," "remember it," "investigate it," "recite it," "retain it," "understand it deeply," "write it down," "penetrate its depths," "incorporate it into one's own life," "teach it," and "honor it," and that we do all of this without the arrogance of egocentricity and possessiveness (96–102).

Having been asked to "accept it" and "believe it," we might be tempted to ask whether the sutra's author would have encouraged us to read it critically, to engage in critical thinking by following our doubts and suspicions to their own conclusions. Perhaps. Although the rhetoric of modern critical thinking would have been unfamiliar, the author might very well have approved. After all, the author had purposefully conjured a literary character—Vimalakirti—who was optimally skilled as a critical thinker. Throughout the sutra he confronts his contemporaries in all honesty, raising serious questions about the coherence and depth of their engagement with the dharma.

Vimalakirti doesn't hold back, often to the point of embarrassing his fellow Buddhists. His criticisms upend the standard piety of the day. He speaks adamantly against the habitual dogmas that some Buddhists repeat without reflection, and he does so without softening the radical edge of that critique. Vimalakirti seeks to elevate everyone's understanding of the dharma. He doesn't suffer fools with bland ideologies supporting bland practices that then give rise to bland and sleepy Buddhists. So yes, we can say with some confidence that the author of the sutra was an admirer of what we call critical thinking.

But critical thinking in pursuit of what? On behalf of what purposes, for what reasons, and in what relationship to the sutra? If, as contemporary readers, we turn to the sutra already positioned as ardent "believers," ready to accept whatever it appears to advise, we will not yet be fulfilling the sutra's admonition "to investigate it," "to understand it deeply," "to penetrate its depths," because asking ourselves rigorously and in all honesty whether what it says is really true is a basic dimension of in-depth understanding. Or, setting aside the question of "belief" and "disbelief" altogether, our modern inclinations might be to read the sutra with particular historical and cultural questions in mind. We might read it, for example, to understand the way the Buddha is represented in it, or the kinds of gender relations assumed in the sutra, or the understanding of literacy that the author presupposed in writing it, or what first-century Buddhists thought about any number of issues.

Even though that rationale and those purposes would be tangential to the rationale and purposes that the sutra recommends, the results may still be of value. But on this approach, we neutralize ourselves and treat the sutra as being about other people in some other time and place, not about us. From the sutra's perspective that leaves out an essential component. If we keep our purposes and our perspectives safely out of view—since this isn't at all about us—we will have essentially immunized ourselves against any existentially serious encounter with the sutra, which, for the sutra, is the whole point, its only reason for being a sutra. Reading it as though it is meant for others in some other time and place—not for us—we keep ourselves hidden in the background, safely protected from Vimalakirti's relentless questioning. In doing that, our own purposes and perspectives are unlikely to be brought out into critical awareness by a wide-open and honest encounter with Vimalakirti's purposes.

Maybe that's why the sutra asks us not just to "read it" and "investigate it" but also to "accept it" and "believe it." We're not asked to believe it without evidence or critical investigation; instead we are asked to seek our own belief on the matter through rigorous inquiry and deep understanding. "Believing," in this sense, would only be possible if we have taken it seriously in the first place, asking ourselves whether or not we agree that the life purposes recommended by the sutra are also the ones that we should be pursuing in our lives. The meditative reading suggested by the sutra would have us investigate and raise questions about what it says while treating it as a serious possibility, something that could conceivably be of value to us in our lives. This open posture would require that on occasion we relinquish our preferred role as inquisitors by allowing the sutra to question us, bringing our own views into play. Stepping back in mindfulness from an unconscious instinct to remain in control, we allow our own values to be placed in juxtaposition to Vimalakirti's so that the sutra might be given an opportunity to speak to us directly, even question us, on issues that it takes to be of ultimate importance. Reading it from the aloof position of investigative oversight, interrogating it, rather than engaging it two-way dialogue lowers the stakes considerably. It avoids Vimalakirti's challenge by taking our own purposes to be beyond question.

So, what are the guiding purposes of the *Vimalakīrti Sūtra*? The sutra aspires to broaden readers' horizons, to provide a more comprehensive perspective on life in hopes that this vision will elevate our aims—the purposes we pursue—and help develop the life skills and dexterity at our disposal for that pursuit. It seeks to inspire us to undertake a path of practice by consciously forming a "thought of enlightenment," a carefully honed image of the kind of life each of us thinks it would be best to live. The sutra wants to inspire extensive meditation on that image so that the image has a chance to assume the role of an "ultimate concern," a concern so central to one's life that it integrates all other concerns into a life-altering journey.

The sutra's author knew that this concern couldn't possibly be ultimate if it was just about you, your well-being. Therefore, central to its thought of enlightenment is the bodhisattva vow to overcome debilitating suffering and enhance life for oneself and everyone else collectively. It recommends learning how to serve as a "benefactor of all living beings" (39) by "overcoming the possessiveness," the "habits of 'I' and 'mine,'" that so easily narrow and imprison our lives.

Vimalakirti was created in great detail as one image of this ideal, one that is broadly applicable since he was an ordinary citizen rather than a religious professional. The sutra describes Vimalakirti as having disciplined himself on the path of wisdom and compassion through the formation and constant guidance of *bodhicitta*, a thought of enlightenment based on a vow of open inclusivity. It shows Vimalakirti putting this conviction into practice through the rigorous discipline of the *pāramitās*, six dimensions of self-overcoming aimed at wisdom, compassion, and skillful means. The sutra's purpose is to persuade you that such a path of wisdom and compassion directed toward an awakened community is the path of purpose that you really ought to be on.

The hope written into the fabric of the sutra is that we readers will consider that image of life, that we will investigate it and understand it to the point that we are provoked by it, and that our own life, our own values, might be brought into critical view in comparison. The sutra was written in the hope that this image of Vimalakirti's path would inspire readers to raise serious existential questions and to set out on a transformative path of their own.

In our own reading of the sutra we should hope that Vimalakirti can do to us what the sutra shows him doing to almost everyone in the narrative—casting doubt on entrenched beliefs and habitual practices, exposing dogmatic clinging, and jolting us into self-examination, thus creating an urgent need for a fundamental overhaul of our sleepy, unawakened ways of being in the world. We should read it in hopes that the motivations and aims that have guided our lives are brought to conscious awareness and open questioning. We should hope that our perspectives are exposed in the light of more comprehensive, more self-aware perspectives. We should hope that the encounter with it alters and elevates our self-conception, the way we understand who we are and what we're doing in life.

Of course, we can't make this happen. But we know from experience that it won't happen unless we cultivate an openness to that possibility. We also sense, of course, that there is risk in that level of personal exposure. Anxieties and failures of various kinds loom. We are far more comfortable avoiding existential risks of this kind than facing them directly. But throughout the sutra Vimalakirti challenges us to forgo the priority of comfort, to be "fearless," "not to be intimidated," and never to settle for "inferior aspirations" because, as the bodhisattva of wisdom explained, "without going out onto the great ocean it is impossible to find precious, priceless pearls" (66).

If there are "priceless pearls" to be found in the *Vimalakīrti Sūtra*, acquiring them would require taking its challenge seriously. In the act of accepting his challenge, Vimalakirti's friends were rendered speechless, thrown back upon their lives for reexamination and realignment. It seems fitting, then, that we end this tribute to Vimalakirti with the hope that at least once in our lives we too might be rendered speechless, for once silencing our chattering avoidances so that a thunderous bolt of lightning might truly wake us up to the extraordinary reality that we are right now living.

English Translations of the *Vimalakīrti Sūtra*

We are fortunate to have six full translations of the *Vimalakīrti Sūtra* into English:

Cleary, Thomas. *Vimalakīrti's Advice.* Amazon.com Services LLC, 2013. (This is a translation from the recently discovered Sanskrit version of the sutra.)

Lamotte, Etienne. *The Teaching of Vimalakirti (Vimalakirtinirdesa).* The Pali Text Society. 1976. (Translated from the French of Lamotte into English by Sara Boin.)

Luk, Charles. *Ordinary Enlightenment: A Translation of the Vimalakirti Nirdesa.* Shambhala Publications, 1975. (Translated from the Chinese version of Kumārajīva, this is the first translation of the sutra to appear in English.)

McRae, John. *Vimalakīrti Sūtra.* Published in conjunction with Diana Paul, *The Sutra of Queen Srimala of the Lion's Roar.* Numata Center for Buddhist Translation and Research, 2004. (An excellent translation from the Chinese of Kumārajīva.)

Thurman, Robert. *The Holy Teaching of Vimalakirti: A Mahayana Scripture.* The Pennsylvania State University Press, 1976. (Translated from Tibetan in consultation with Chinese versions, this is an excellent translation, the one used throughout this book.)

Watson, Burton. *The Vimalakirti Sutra.* Columbia University Press, 1997. (Another translation from the Chinese of Kumārajīva by one of the premier translators of Chinese classics.)